The Political Economy of Trade Finance

AF839595

Export Credit Agencies provide insurance and guarantees to domestic firms in the event that payment is not received from an importer. Thus, ECAs reduce uncertainties domestic firms face in exporting their goods. Most countries have ECAs that operate as official or quasi-official branches of their governments and they therefore represent an important part of government strategies to facilitate trade, promote domestic industry and distribute foreign aid.

The Political Economy of Trade Finance provides a detailed analysis as to how firms use the medium and longer-term financing provided by ECAs to export goods to developing countries. It also explains how ECA arrears have contributed to the debt of developing countries and illustrates how the commercial interests of ECA activity are evident in decisions about IMF arrangements and related to Paris Club debt rescheduling agreements. Finally, the book documents how the medium and longer-term export credit insurance support provided by the G-7 ECAs was a central component in mitigating steep declines in international trade during the 2008 Global Financial Crisis. This book is of great interest to both academics and students in the field of political economy, finance and politics of international trade. It is also of importance to policy makers.

Pamela Blackmon is Associate Professor at the Department of Political Science, Pennsylvania State University, Altoona, USA. Her research focuses on policies of the international financial institutions, and she is currently examining the role of ECAs in international trade and finance.

Routledge Frontiers of Political Economy

For a full list of titles in this series please visit www.routledge.com/books/series/SE0345

217. **Creative Research in Economics**
   Arnold Wentzel

218. **The Economic Ideas of Marx's Capital**
   Steps towards post-Keynesian economics
   Ludo Cuyvers

219. **A New Economics for Modern Dynamic Economies**
   Innovation, uncertainty and entrepreneurship
   Angelo Fusari

220. **Income Distribution and Environmental Sustainability**
   A Sraffian approach
   Robin Hahnel

221. **The Creation of Wealth and Poverty**
   Means and ways
   Hassan Bougrine

222. **Labour Managed Firms and Post-Capitalism**
   Bruno Jossa

223. **New Financial Ethics**
   A Normative Approach
   Aloy Soppe

224. **The Political Economy of Trade Finance**
   Export Credit Agencies, the Paris Club and the IMF
   Pamela Blackmon

The Political Economy of Trade Finance

Export Credit Agencies, the Paris Club and the IMF

Pamela Blackmon

Routledge
Taylor & Francis Group
LONDON AND NEW YORK

First published 2017 by Routledge

2 Park Square, Milton Park, Abingdon, Oxfordshire OX14 4RN
52 Vanderbilt Avenue, New York, NY 10017

Routledge is an imprint of the Taylor & Francis Group, an informa business

First issued in paperback 2019

British Library Cataloguing in Publication Data
A catalogue record for this book is available from the British Library

Library of Congress Cataloging in Publication Data
A catalog record for this book has been requested

ISBN: 978-1-138-78056-9 (hbk)
ISBN: 978-0-367-87016-4 (pbk)

Typeset in Sabon
by Swales & Willis Ltd, Exeter, Devon, UK

Brief contents

Detailed contents

Figures

Tables

Abbreviations

BAFT	Bankers' Association for Finance and Trade
BRIC	Brazil, Russia, India and China
CLS	Country Limitation Schedule
DAC	Development Assistance Committee
DSA	Debt Sustainability Assessment
EB	Executive Board
ECA	Export Credit Agency
ECF	Extended Credit Facility
ECGD	Export Credits Guarantee Department
ED	Executive Directors
EDC	Export Development Corporation
EFF	Extended Fund Facility
E-HIPC	Enhanced Heavily Indebted Poor Countries
ESAF	Enhanced Structural Adjustment Facility
Ex-Im Bank	Export-Import Bank
EU	European Union
FY	Fiscal Year
GDP	Gross Domestic Product
GFC	Global Financial Crisis
GNI	Gross National Income
HIPC	Heavily Indebted Poor Countries
IBRD	International Bank for Reconstruction and Development
ICC	International Chamber of Commerce
IDA	International Development Association
IEO	Independent Evaluation Office
IFI	International Financial Institution
IGO	Intergovernmental Organization
IMF	International Monetary Fund
JBIC	Japanese Bank for International Cooperation

MDGs	Millennium Development Goals
MDRI	Multilateral Development Relief Initiative
MIGA	Multilateral Investment Guarantee Agency
MONA	Monitoring of Fund Arrangements
NGO	Non-governmental organization
NPV	Net Present Value
ODA	Official Development Assistance
OECD	Organization for Economic Cooperation and Development
OPEC	Organization of the Petroleum Exporting Countries
PF	Project Finance
PNG	private non-guaranteed
PPG	public and publicly guaranteed
PRGF	Poverty Reduction and Growth Facility
PRI	Political Risk Insurance
PRSP	Poverty Reduction Strategy Paper
PSI	Policy Support Instrument
PV	Present Value
RBS	Royal Bank of Scotland
SACE	Servizi Assicurativi del Commercio Estero
SBA	Stand-By Arrangement
UNDP	United Nations Development Program

Acknowledgments

I have many people to thank for their assistance with this book. First, I would like to thank Robert Langham, who was the Economics Editor at Routledge and whom I first contacted about this book proposal. His enthusiastic support of the project was most welcome. I would also like to thank Andy Humphries and the anonymous reviewers for their comments and suggestions. I would also like to thank all of the economists at the US Export-Import Bank who have spoken with me over the years, and especially William Marsteller, who often suggested people I should talk to regarding export credit support during the 2008 crisis. I very much appreciate your time and willingness to share your insights with me. Delio Gianturco, Fabrice Morel, Erin Hannah, Andrew Moravcsik, Samuel Barkin, Tina Zappile, Stephanie Rickard, Pablo Toral, Thomas Willett, Noel Johnston, Enrique Coscio-Pascal, Lex Rieffel and Scott Cooper all provided comments and suggestions during different stages of this project. Makayla Zonfrilli, Justin Girven, Clayton Lukes and Arianna Henderson provided excellent research and logistical support for the project as my undergraduate research assistants. I would also like to thank the students over the years in two of my courses: "Globalization and Its Impacts" and "Controversies in International Relations" who patiently sat through my presentations on export credit agencies, and their role in trade finance.

I would like to acknowledge the financial and institutional support that I received for this project. My fellowship from the Institute for the Arts and Humanities, Pennsylvania State University, University Park, allowed me to devote time and energy to writing and provided a supportive and collegial environment under which to do so. The Office of Research and Sponsored Programs, Pennsylvania State University, Altoona, has supported my research with many, many trips to Washington, DC, over the years so that I could carry out research and conduct various interviews. I am very grateful for the

Research and Development Grants which supported my research. I also thank Taylor & Francis for permission to reprint some material from "Determinants of Developing Country Debt: the Revolving Door of Debt Rescheduling through the Paris Club and Export Credits" and I thank John Wiley & Sons for permission to reprint some material from "Global Companies, the Bretton Woods Institutions and Global Justice" in the Handbook of Global Companies.

My family has always provided encouragement and support, which I very much appreciate. My parents Betty and Bill Lyle and my in-laws Marty and Judy Freedman have always supported my research and asked "How is the book coming?" My husband, Jason Freedman really encouraged me to write this book, even though after the first book I said I would not be writing a second one for a long, long time. This is an indication that he knows me pretty well. Jason is a great reviewer for me because he will tell me when a particular sentence "put him to sleep" which is important information for an author to know. I was pregnant with my second son Eli, during the summer of 2010 when I first went to talk to US Export-Import Bank economists to find out if export credit agency support had been used during the financial crisis. Thus, Eli has really been with me from the very beginning of the project!

I hope that this area of research is the beginning of an opportunity for political scientists to uncover an area of political economy that is severely understudied: trade finance. Maybe this book will provide the impetus to move my colleagues to undertake the study of export credit, and export credit agencies more fully. Nevertheless, as I always tell my children, perseverance means pushing ahead to do something that you feel passionately about *especially* when it is difficult.

Introduction

On May 29, 2014 Argentina concluded a Paris Club debt rescheduling agreement. This was a noteworthy accomplishment since the country had been a virtual pariah since defaulting on its debt in 2001. As a result of the commitment of Argentina to pay its arrears to the Paris Club creditors and normalize financial relations, the Press Release confirmed, "Paris Club members' export credit agencies that wish to do so will resume their export credit activities" (Paris Club Press Release May 29, 2014). This agreement was noted by one economist as being immediately significant since it would allow Argentina to benefit from trade financing from the export credit agencies of the Paris Club (Mander 2014). What are the connections between Paris Club rescheduling and Export Credit Agencies (ECAs)? The purpose of this book is to explain how ECAs mitigate contemporary risks inherent in international trade by providing trade insurance, and to analyze how ECAs contribute to the political economy of trade finance.

There are many risks in international trade, and the provision of trade insurance as a way to mitigate those risks has been around for centuries, with early examples including Lloyd's of London (1688) and the offering of marine insurance by the Dutch East India Company (de Vries and van der Woude 1997). Indeed, one of the more prominent forms of non-life insurance was marine insurance because it "helped the Europeans protect their long and arduous sea journeys, beset by storms, shipwreck and pirates, in order to satisfy their appetite for spices, coffee, sugar, and cotton" (Borscheid and Viggo Haueter 2012: 4). As industrialization and the economic revolution progressed, these risks were understood as part of the process in increasing opportunities for business. Since the end of the eighteenth century, the insurance industry expanded based on an increased willingness to take on risk; and risk began to be seen as a challenge that could be managed instead of as a threat (Borscheid and Viggo Haueter 2012: 4, 5). Managing trade risks is a role filled by export credit insurers that are "as much a symbol of global integration as marine insurance and reinsurance" (Borscheid and Viggo Haueter 2012: 64).

Contemporary risks in international trade include the problems inherent in the transport of goods in the examples cited above, but today's risks more often involve problems in payments for goods received. ECAs provide insurance for two main categories of risk: political risk, when a government does not honor a contract (also called sovereign risk); and commercial risk, when a private buyer or commercial bank does not pay for goods. There are many types of political risk insurance that firms can choose from such as insuring against nonconvertibility of currency, expropriation or nationalization, war and civil war, breach of contract and cancellation of licenses (Stephens 1999; MIGA Staff 2010). For example, firms exporting goods to the government of Uzbekistan would likely use political insurance to protect against transfer and currency convertibility restrictions in the country since there have been problems with converting the country's domestic currency back into dollars (Blackmon 2011). Since economic sanctions were lifted against Iran in January 2016, many European oil services firms have shown interest in investing in Iranian oil and gas fields. These are large infrastructure and development projects with a country that has engaged in expropriation or nationalization in the past, and these firms will likely take out political risk insurance against those actions. Commercial risk insurance applies to the private sector and the types of insurance firms can choose from include insolvency, bankruptcy or failure to take delivery of goods (repudiation) (Stephens 1999: 76). Thus, the main purpose of ECAs is to reduce the uncertainty and risk inherent in international trade by providing insurance to mitigate those risks.

Political and economic considerations of ECAs are relevant to political scientists because most governments have ECAs that operate as official or quasi-official branches of their governments. The G-7 states (the US, the UK, Canada, France, Japan, Germany and Italy) and most of the countries in the Organization for Economic Cooperation and Development (OECD) have ECAs. Export credit insurers are either public insurers, which are official ECAs that have their financing backed by their respective governments, or private insurers which operate commercially in order to make a profit for their shareholders (Morel 2010: 9). However, these are not clear distinctions since even private credit insurers such as Germany's Euler Hermes and France's Coface only provide medium and longer-term coverage in risky markets on the basis of support from their respective governments. This means, in effect, that the business the agency underwrites is on behalf of its government, and that the government would fund claim payments (Stephens 1999: 88). ECAs represent an important part of government strategies to facilitate trade and promote domestic industry exports.

Surprisingly, there is little scholarly attention paid to the role of ECAs in facilitating international trade in the political science literature. Andrew Moravcsik's (1989: 174) early article on the OECD Export Credit Arrangement examined "the Arrangement" as an international regime which set up rules among member states, ECAs in order to govern "one of the most widely employed instruments of state export promotion: subsidized trade finance." He provides a historical account as to how the Arrangement was negotiated as well as positing that the success of the regime over time (it was created in 1975) has been due to international cooperation fostered by the structure of government institutions (Moravcsik 1989: 174–5). More recently, Christopher Wright (2011) reviewed how ECAs have been "highly" influential in increasing trade in the energy sector through promoting national exports to countries with high political risks. In one of Eric Helleiner's (2011: 69) articles about the 2008 Global Financial Crisis, he does mention the fact that international trade credits decreased during the crisis, and that this affected trade, but his article more clearly details the degree to which International Political Economy (IPE) scholars anticipated the crisis.

By and large, it has been economists and those involved in export insurance and finance that have examined the role of ECAs and trade finance. A number of scholars that have worked for ECAs, notably the US Export-Import Bank, have written about these topics. For example, Delio Gianturco (2001: 1) proclaims "the world's export credit agencies (are) the 'unsung giants' of international finance" The volume on the relevance of the US Export-Import Bank (and ECAs in general) edited by Gary Clyde Haufbauer and Rita Rodriguez (2001) (Rodriguez worked for the US Export-Import Bank) is the most comprehensive in dealing with the various issues faced by ECAs including some chapters that touch on the political problems of government-supported trade finance (Niskanen 2001; Summers 2001). Janet Koven Levit (2004) follows Moravcsik's analysis of the OECD Export credit Arrangement and shows empirically that ECAs consistently comply with the rules of the Arrangement even though it is not a formal treaty, and its members are not bound by international law. Finally, Andreas Klasen (2011) who is the Head of Export and Investment Finance for PricewaterhouseCoopers, documented the role that public ECAs played in maintaining trade flows during the 2008 financial crisis.

Indeed, the global nature of the 2008 financial crisis and the degree to which trade is supported by trade finance has resulted in economists reexamining the study of ECAs and their role in trade finance. Economists found, for example, that the scarce availability of trade credit could be responsible for the decrease in the volume of exports (Amiti and Weinstein 2009; Auboin 2009; Asmundson, Dorsey, Khachatryan, Niculcea and Saito 2011). During the crisis ECAs increased their short-term export credit insurance cover for transactions with repayment terms of less than two years due to the reduction in short-term support provided by private insurers (Morel 2010; Klasen 2011). The increased involvement of ECAs in the short-term resulted from the withdrawal of the private sector from this type of cover as a result of the crisis and is not expected to be a long-term trend. However, ECAs also increased their medium and longer-term support during this crisis, which is the focus of Chapter 5 in this book.

While economists, and those involved in export credit insurance and finance, have covered the topic of trade finance and its role in facilitating trade, there has been little work done by political scientists on the implications of government-supported trade finance. In this book I hope to bridge the gap between the coverage of this topic by economists and its lack of coverage from IPE. The field of IPE seeks to understand the interconnectedness of politics and economics in a number of areas including the study of international organizations, international trade and international finance (Gilpin 1994; Helleiner 2011). This theoretical framework is useful for an analysis of government-supported trade finance because there are two institutions that involve decisions about how those resources are allocated through state-supported ECAs: the Paris Club and the International Monetary Fund (IMF). Specifically, I will be analyzing how government-supported trade finance through ECAs is an important component in Paris Club debt rescheduling agreements and indirectly through decisions about IMF arrangements.

The IMF is involved in this process because a debtor country is required to be under an IMF arrangement before a Paris Club debt rescheduling agreement. In fact, the Paris Club rescheduling agreement with Argentina on May 29, 2014 in which Argentina was able to proceed with rescheduling without an IMF arrangement, and without the IMF as an observer to the agreement, was unprecedented. According to a report in Business News Americas, the creditors agreed to let Argentina proceed without an IMF arrangement in return for a larger down payment (Levy 2014). In the past, Nigeria was able to proceed without an IMF arrangement that would provide financial support and the IMF developed a specific instrument for this situation with Nigeria, called the Policy Support Instrument (PSI), which will be discussed further in Chapter 4. Under a PSI a country has an agreement with the IMF even though the country does not need to avail itself of IMF financial support. According to the Paris Club Press Release, Argentina agreed to clear arrears within five years including a minimum of $1,150 million to be paid by May 2015 with the following payment due May 2016.[1] The following section will provide an overview of the Paris Club and how its activities involve the rescheduling of debt from ECAs.

The Paris Club

The Paris Club is a term used to signify an informal group of creditor countries that meet to defer or reschedule payment obligations from debtor countries that are unable to meet their payment obligations (Rieffel 1985). There are currently 20 "permanent members" of the Paris Club, and all but two, the Russian Federation and Israel, are members of the OECD.[2] These members represent the states with the largest exposure to other countries, although other creditor countries can be invited to participate in negotiations with debtor countries if they choose to have their debt rescheduled. Each time that a country concludes a Paris Club rescheduling agreement, creditor countries that participated in the rescheduling are listed along with "observers" which always include representatives from the IMF and the World Bank and can include representatives from organizations such as UNCTAD and the European Commission (Rieffel 2003: 64–65). In most of the agreements, the creditor countries include the G-7 states plus the Netherlands and Switzerland, since they are the states with the largest exposure. The Netherlands is often included as a participating creditor because its ECA, Atradius, is one of the biggest private insurers in the world (Van der Veer 2011: 202). Since only creditor countries that choose to participate in the rescheduling procedures of debtor countries are included in the agreement for a particular country, it means that not all Paris Club members participate in the rescheduling procedures of debtor countries. This "flexible participation" by creditor countries explains why the Paris Club is referred to as an informal group of countries even though it has permanent members.

Lex Rieffel (1985: 3) who has engaged in the most extensive research on the Paris Club, explains that the best way to categorize the Paris Club is that it is a "set of *procedures* currently used for negotiating arrangements to defer payment obligations on credits extended or guaranteed by creditor-country government agencies to both public-sector and private-sector borrowers in debtor countries" (emphasis in original). In many cases, these debt obligations were from credits that were either extended or guaranteed by creditor country government agencies, which are often ECAs. For example, Rieffel (1985: 2–3) provides criteria on the types of credits that are involved in Paris Club negotiations: credits from official institutions granted to public and private sector entities; credits from private lenders that carry a guarantee of repayment from an official agency (such as the US Export-Import Bank (his example); finally, a guarantee from any official creditor-country agency means that the credit will be rescheduled during Paris Club procedures.

Thomas Callaghy (2002: 14) explains that the Paris Club "is a complex and powerful hybrid international organization, one that reveals a lot about the evolution of the international political economy and the nature of its governance processes." Research on Paris Club negotiations has focused on the debt restructuring agreements themselves (Cheru 2006), and the fact that the debt of many countries has been rescheduled repeatedly (Boorman 2006). In fact, it is rare for a country to only conclude one debt rescheduling agreement with the Paris Club. According to data from the Paris Club, there have been 430 rescheduling agreements since 1956 but with only 90 different debtor countries.[3] Thus, not much of the literature on Paris Club negotiations is focused on the origins of country debt and the fact that much of it is comprised of ECA debt. While Eurodad (2011) correctly notes that almost 80 percent of poor countries' debts to European governments came from export credits and not from development loans, there is only an occasional mention of Paris Club negotiations in this study. Nor are there discussions in the IPE literature about the political and economic implications of creditor country government involvement in these two areas of trade finance: extending export credit facilities through their ECAs and the subsequent rescheduling of this debt in the Paris Club.

The IMF

The involvement of the IMF is an important component in the political economy of trade finance for two interrelated reasons. First, as mentioned previously, a debtor country must be under an IMF arrangement before Paris Club negotiations can proceed. The Paris Club debt rescheduling process involves the IMF more directly than the World Bank because "[a]s a precondition to Paris Club negotiations, the creditors insist that the debtor country conclude an appropriate arrangement with the IMF" (Rieffel 1985: 8). This is deemed to be necessary because the creditors want assurances that the required policy reforms will allow the country to be able to service its debts completely and on schedule, and going through the IMF is believed to be the best way to get these assurances (Rieffel 1985: 7–8). While it is not surprising that creditor countries require a debtor country to have an IMF arrangement in place prior to Paris Club negotiations, it is surprising that this requirement is not discussed as part of the vast IPE literature on political and economic determinants of IMF loans.

Richard Brown (1992) provides a comprehensive analysis of the conflicting role between the involvement of the IMF and Paris Club debt rescheduling. His article addresses what he sees (rightly) to be a problem with the situation that the IMF is forgoing its role as "guardian of economic policy reform" by entering into these "functional policy agreements" in cases where governments may not be able to adhere to the criteria in them (Brown 1992: 291–292). Specifically, he states:

> creditor government concern with speedy debt relief (through Paris Club Debt rescheduling procedures) can, in some instances, bring pressure to bear on the IMF to reach a credit agreement without insisting on the usual policy conditionality, or to draw up a programme that it knows is unlikely to be carried out by the debtor government.
>
> (Brown 1992: 292)

Brown finds that there is a relationship between an increased role by the IMF in mediating debt rescheduling agreements between debtor countries (especially low-income sub-Saharan African countries) and creditor governments in the Paris Club, and increased "slippage" in IMF conditionality agreements. In other words, he argues that this was a pattern in which the IMF has lost some of its leverage in getting debtor countries to comply with conditionality criteria and that these countries were becoming even more indebted. This led to a worsening economic situation, whereby the countries became ineligible for IMF credit further reducing the likelihood that they would follow program criteria (Sachs 1989; Brown 1992). Brown seeks to call attention to the fact that the IMF has "multiple roles in the world economy" and that it does not solely function in the manner under which it was designed. Recent literature on IMF lending and conditionality criteria has certainly addressed the "multiple roles" that the IMF plays especially regarding relationships between loans as a way to meet political and economic goals of its important member states (Copelovitch 2010a, b; Stone 2011; Dreher, Strum and Vreeland 2013). Although, this literature has not addressed how the requirement of an IMF arrangement prior to Paris Club rescheduling has important economic implications for creditor states that want to resume lending to debtor countries through their ECAs.

Thus, the second interrelated reason as to why the IMF is an important component in understanding the political economy of trade finance has to do with the necessity of the rescheduling of old debt under Paris Club agreements prior to the resumption of new ECA activity. This is called the "subordination strategy" and means that only after old loans are restructured, can countries then be eligible for new credits in the form of guarantees or insurance in support of new export loans (Kuhn 1994: 24). Indeed, the May 2014 agreement between Argentina and the Paris Club on debt repayment was important because it would allow Argentina to qualify once again for export credit facilities (Paris Club Press Release May 29, 2014).

In Chapter 4, I argue that there is a relationship between creditor country involvement in decisions made about IMF loans, Paris Club debt rescheduling and the extension of new export credit facilities to debtor countries. The process can be summed up as follows: an IMF arrangement is required for Paris Club rescheduling (which is part of the motivation for an IMF arrangement) along with Paris Club rescheduling being completed so that debtor countries do not fall into arrears, a situation that would prevent the extension of new export credits. However, the creditor countries that often extend new export credits through their ECAs are also in decision-making positions in the IMF and the Paris Club. There is one other component in the process of IMF programs and Paris Club rescheduling agreements that is under analyzed in the broader IPE literature: the Heavily Indebted Poor Countries Initiative (HIPC).

The HIPC and Paris Club rescheduling

The Heavily Indebted Poor Countries Initiative (HIPC), developed in 1996, represented fundamental changes to debt forgiveness for highly indebted poor countries because for the first time debt relief would be provided by the multilateral creditors of the IMF and the World Bank, in addition to other multilateral development banks (Gupta, Clements, Guin Siu and Leruth 2004). Prior to this, debt relief had been provided through reductions on the debt of low-income countries through the

Paris Club beginning in 1988 under Toronto terms, and through initiatives by bilateral donors to offer grants instead of highly concessional loans (Birdsall, Williams and Deese 2002: 22–23). These programs succeeded in reducing the debt owed from HIPC countries to their bilateral creditors but "by the mid 1990s an increasing proportion of the debt of the poorest countries was owed to official multilateral creditors, notably the IMF and World Bank" (Birdsall, Williams and Deese 2002: 23–24). The HIPC Initiative with debt forgiveness from the multilaterals was deemed necessary because these countries still had high debt levels after programs of debt relief from other creditors had been implemented. While HIPC involves multilateral debt forgiveness for the first time, the process also includes Paris Club creditor debt in debt forgiveness.

In addition, in some cases this "forgiveness", or debt cancellation, is an accounting transaction whereby the forgiven amount is transferred from development agencies to creditor country ECAs in order to repay the debts. In the study, done by Eurodad (2011: 3, 26), they found that 85 percent of bilateral debts cancelled from 2005 to 2009 from European ECAs of the Netherlands, the UK, Sweden, Belgium and Switzerland were debts resulting from export credit guarantees. Norway's ECA was not included since the country does not report bilateral debt cancellation as Official Development Assistance (ODA). For example, in the 2004–2005 Annual Report of the UK's ECA, the Export Credits Guarantee Department (ECGD) it is noted with regard to countries under the HIPC Initiative:

> [a]s long as they remain on track with their IMF/WB supported programmes, the UK will agree to forgiveness of their debt and the Department for International Development will pay ECGD on their behalf. At HIPC Completion Point, the debt stock is irrevocably and unconditionally written off.
>
> (United Kingdom, ECGD 2004–05 Annual Report: 15)

There has been a vast amount of literature as to whether the HIPC process is substantially different than previous debt relief initiatives in reducing the debt of low-income countries (Easterly 2001, 2006; Cheru 2006). These issues will be addressed in more detail in Chapter 3, but there are two bigger issues regarding the debt relief process that have been overlooked. The first issue is that it seems much of the debt "forgiveness" is actually taken out of development assistance money that would have been used for the debtor countries and is instead going to pay their previous or old ECA loans. In fact, one of the criticisms of the

HIPC process is the argument that many countries are not paying this nonconcessional debt anyway, thus the idea that debt payments can be re-directed toward poverty alleviating initiatives does not work if the money was not first allocated toward debt repayment in the first place (Easterly 2001; Weiss 2008). This argument does have some merit with regard to Paris Club serial rescheduling of debt, although not with regard to the multilateral creditors of the IMF and World Bank since they are treated as preferred creditors, meaning that their credit is universally recognized "as senior to all other debt" (Birdsall et al. 2002: 25). Thus, while it does seem to be the case that there is not as much money available to re-direct toward poverty alleviating initiatives (as was the requirement under the Enhanced Heavily Indebted Poor Countries (E-HIPC) Initiative), there is not much written about the fact that some countries are actually losing money from the payment of previous export credit debts when debt forgiveness comes out of ODA funds. As noted by Eurodad (2011: 2):

> [c]ounting debt cancellation as ODA is comparable to creative accounting: debts owed by developing countries which were often only on the books and that creditors were not even hoping to recover are suddenly counted as part of the donors' commitments . . . all OECD countries (except Norway) report debt relief to developing countries as part of governments' development aid.

The second issue that is generally overlooked is that the amount of HIPC Paris Club debt is rather large even when compared to HIPC debt owed to the multilateral creditors. In other words, the argument that the amount of debt relief provided under HIPC is small may be true as regards to multilateral debt but it is not the case regarding Paris Club debt. The World Bank provides estimates of the potential costs of the HIPC Initiative borne by eight creditor groups: World Bank; IMF; AFDB Group; IADB; Other Multilateral Creditors; Paris Club; Other Official Bilateral and Commercial. Not only was the Paris Club the creditor group with the highest potential costs (in Present Value (PV) terms) for end-2009, end-2011 and end-2012 but the potential costs estimated to be borne by the Paris Club increased from end-2009 at 36 percent (or $27.1 billion) to end-2011 at 36.3 percent (or $27.6 billion). The most recent data indicates that the cost of Paris Club debt, but not the percentage of debt, decreased slightly for end-2012 at 36.3 percent (or $27 billion).[4]

On the one hand much of this Paris Club debt is comprised of ECA debt owed to the creditor governments, although some Paris Club debt is also ODA debt. On the other hand, it appears that Paris Club debt forgiveness is not that big of a deal either in the sense that it is providing a tremendous amount of debt forgiveness (for debtor countries) or in the sense that creditor country governments are actually losing money from the debt forgiveness. If most creditor countries are simply subtracting from development assistance money it is unclear apart from interest on the debt exactly how much "debt forgiveness" is involved. In addition, creditor country governments are able to continue to export their goods abroad and some HIPC countries (such as Ghana, Cameroon and Honduras) benefitted from subsequent ECA activity from the ECAs of the US, the UK and Canada after reaching the HIPC completion point. Clearly these issues are important to our understanding of the political economy of trade finance and the role that the Paris Club, the IMF and World Bank play in these processes, and will be addressed more fully in Chapter 3.

Overview and structure of the book

I conducted many interviews with US Export-Import Bank (US Ex-Im Bank) economists and officials that will be cited throughout this book. In the course of a telephone conversation and subsequent e-mail correspondence with a former US Ex-Im Bank Director, this person posed a question "As a political scientist, how did you get interested in the ECA world?" (Personal correspondence with the author, May 11, 2012). A more pertinent question is, "Why *aren't* political scientists more aware of the activity surrounding ECAs?" Certainly the field of political science with its focus on the study of governments, political processes and systems in addition to the field of political economy can find much to study and analyze in the world of trade finance.

The book is organized as follows: Chapter 1 provides background information on ECAs including the theoretical framework for the book explaining why ECAs are necessary in order to facilitate international trade. This chapter will also explain the differences between the two primary institutions involved in export credit activity: the International Union of Credit and Investment Insurers (also known as the Berne Union) and the Export Credits Division of the Organization for Economic Cooperation and Development (OECD). The Berne Union is the largest group of credit insurers and operates more as an association with "guiding principles" for public and private ECAs. OECD states that are Participants to the Arrangement on Officially Supported Export Credits (the Arrangement) use their officially-backed ECAs to "provide a framework for the orderly use of official export credits" for a time period of over two years thereby "reducing subsidies and trade distortions related to officially supported export credits" and disclose this information to the OECD Secretariat.[5] This chapter will also show how the Export Credits Division under the Arrangement monitors the export credit activity of its member states.

Chapter 2 focuses on the types of firms that rely on ECAs in order to export their goods to developing countries. The chapter reviews in greater detail the ways in which firms use the trade financing mechanisms of ECAs in order to mitigate the risks of exporting goods to developing countries. Specifically, the chapter identifies the firms in the US, the UK and Canada that have used their respective ECAs (the US Ex-Im Bank, the UK's Export Credits Guarantee Department, and Canada's Export Development Corporation) in order to export goods to developing and/or lower-middle income countries.

Chapter 3 details how ECA debt is rescheduled through the Paris Club and how Official Development Assistance (ODA) is used in debt forgiveness. This chapter also explains in more detail how the HIPC Initiative is a factor in Paris Club rescheduling in two ways. First, developing countries are able to qualify for irrevocable debt relief from creditors including Paris Club creditors, if they reach the completion point under HIPC. Second, empirical evidence is provided to show that debt forgiveness is often subtracted from ODA money lessening the resources that HIPC countries could use for poverty alleviating initiatives.

Chapter 4 provides an empirical analysis of the repetition of IMF loans coupled with the serial rescheduling processes of the Paris Club. I use an original data set of countries that received debt rescheduling from the Paris Club while under an IMF arrangement using data from the ECAs of the US, Canada, Japan and the UK from 2000–2012. I find that after debt rescheduling was completed, that the debtor countries received future export credits or loans from the ECAs of those same creditor countries that rescheduled the debt. These broader interests of promoting trade and encouraging developing countries to reduce trade barriers provide an additional explanation as to why the IMF also continues its process of repeated structural adjustment loans to the same countries since an IMF agreement is required before the Paris Club rescheduling process begins.

Chapter 5 shows how the OECD Participant states would turn to their ECAs in order to provide officially-backed (or government-supported) medium and longer-term export credit insurance cover in order to increase trade during the 2008 Global Financial Crisis.[6] The 2008 financial crisis impacted international trade flows in part because of decreases in both trade finance and export credit insurance. These are common trade mechanisms, although little research on the aspects of increased state involvement in providing export credit insurance has been conducted in the political economy literature.

The final chapter summarizes the main findings and reviews why the use of ECAs as mechanisms to increase trade is likely to increase in the future.

Notes

1 Paris Club Press Release *The Paris Club and the Argentine Republic Agree to a Resumption of Payments and to Clearance of all Arrears* (http://clubdeparis.org/sections/actualites/argentine/downloadFile/PDF/PR20140529_Argentine.pdf?nocache=1401336431.64) and see the May 29, 2014 article in the *Financial Times* 'Argentina Reaches Landmark Deal with Paris Club Creditors' at http://ft.com/cms/s/0/212b0b1e-e722-11e3-aa93-00144feabdc0.html#axzz37SvilfbR).

2 The 20 members are Austria, Australia, Belgium, Canada, Denmark, Finland, France, Germany, Ireland, Israel, Italy, Japan, Netherlands, Norway, Russian Federation, Spain, Sweden, Switzerland, UK and US. Israel became the newest member on June 24, 2014 (http://clubdeparis.org/sections/actualites/etat-d-israel-devient/viewLanguage/en).

3 http://clubdeparis.org/sections/donnees-chiffrees/chiffres-cles

4 Information for 2009 was provided to me from the World Bank. Data for 2011 is available from the World Bank website: http://go.worldbank.org/48MIDC8BH0

5 http://oecd.org/tad/xcred/participants.htm

6 Of the OECD member states the following are Participants to the Arrangement: Australia, Canada, the European Union states, Japan, Korea, New Zealand, Norway, Switzerland and the US. The following OECD member states do not have an ECA and thus are not Participants: Chile, Iceland and Ireland. Mexico is the only OECD member state with an ECA that is not a Participant to the Arrangement (Israel and Turkey are observers to the Participants meetings) (http://oecd.org/tad/xcred/participants.htm).

1 Insuring and financing trade

ECAs promote and facilitate domestic exports. They do this by providing financing through direct lending, or more often through insurance, or guarantees of loans made through private sector finance designed to reduce the risk of nonpayment on exports incurred by domestic export industries. In fact, 80 to 90 percent of trade transactions involve some form of credit, short-term, insurance or guarantee achieved through trade financing (Auboin 2009: 4; WTO 2008). The risk of nonpayment due to the buyer's government is under the category of political (or sovereign) risk that ECAs insure against; specifically these are actions by a government that include civil war, acts of war or preventing the transfer of payments. The second category of risk that ECAs ensure against is commercial (or non-sovereign) risk which is the risk of nonpayment by a private buyer, commercial bank, or public buyer; specifically insolvency, bankruptcy or non-payment (Stephens 1999: 76, 106). For example, the UK established the first governmental ECA in 1919 in order to provide exports to the USSR (lending on a sovereign basis) that would not have occurred under the newly installed communist government. The US Export-Import Bank (Ex-Im Bank) was established in 1934 via decree from US president FDR in order to not lose exports to the USSR especially around the time of the Great Depression (Hufbauer and Rodriguez 2001: 3–4).

Who benefits from ECAs?

Economic theories generally explain that openness to trade is beneficial in the aggregate for states, but that there are diffuse costs depending on the factor endowments and differences in the comparative advantages of states (Stolper and Samuelson 1941). This is often where politics influences the trade policies of a state, on the basis of which groups benefit from trade and which groups are disadvantaged by trade. Workers that do not benefit from trade openness want protectionist policies restricting trade, and workers benefitting from trade support open trade policies (Frieden 2006: 109–111). Workers in a steel mill are harmed by cheaper imports of steel, threatening their jobs. Conversely, Boeing employees understand that Boeing's ability to export planes is crucial to the productivity of the firm, and thus their continued employment. Unsurprisingly, the citizens that are aware of the existence of ECAs are the ones that benefit from them; notably firms that are heavily export-intensive. Previous research has shown that citizens are likely to support trade and that exporters will mobilize in support of trade when those citizens and exporters benefit from increased trade (Kaltenthaler, Gelleny and Ceccoli 2004; Dur 2007). Therefore, there are strong political and economic motivations for governmental leaders and export firms to support exports and by extension export finance (Czinkota 1983; Reid 1983: 130–131). Powerful export industries benefit from this relationship because they have access to some markets that would otherwise have been too costly, and governmental leaders benefit because they are able to boast that financing through these agencies contributes to increasing domestic employment and exports.

Thus, ECAs are somewhat unique in these debates concerning the benefits of trade openness because, since ECAs provide financing support for the export of *domestically manufactured* goods, their trade and export activities would be supported by domestic workers and firms.[1] Export credits are provided for short-term financing (up to two years) for consumer goods and raw materials; medium-term financing for capital goods; and longer-term financing for investment and infrastructure related projects (Kuhn, Horvath and Jarvis 1995: 5, 14). Most ECA credit activity has been for medium and longer-term business because commercial banks covering the risks for these types of projects would charge much higher interest rates than ECAs, so export industries prefer ECA insurance (Gianturco 2001: 2). Commercial banks often do not want to assume the risk period involved in insuring projects of a longer-term nature such as large infrastructure and capital goods projects, investments of sunk capital in which losses would be difficult to recover (Moran 1999; 2006). An additional reason that commercial banks are reluctant to cover medium and longer-term financing is that these longer-term debt obligations are subject to rescheduling in Paris Club debt rescheduling agreements (Cline 2005: 20). Thus, exporters turn to ECAs when private sector insurance is either too expensive or not available (Kuhn et al. 1995: 12, 14).[2] The following sections explain the differences between the two primary institutions involved in export credit activity: the Berne Union and the Organization for Economic Cooperation and Development (OECD).[3]

Export credit under the Berne Union and the OECD

The Berne Union (also known as the International Union of Credit and Investment Insurers) established in 1934, was the first international institution designed to establish rules and principles for export insurance as well as to allow for the discussion and facilitation of information among its members. The Berne Union has grown from the initial four founding member states (the UK, Spain, France and Italy) in 1934 into an astonishing 48 members in 2010. As of 2008, its new business volumes were over US$1.5 trillion; 20 percent above the level recorded in 2007 (Berne Union Yearbook 2009: 11). However, the Berne Union is unique in that while it is comprised of government ECAs, it also has private companies among its membership; the institutions themselves are the members not the governments. In addition, in order to be a member of the Berne Union, the company (or ECA) must provide some type of export insurance or finance. In other words, if the company or bank only provides direct loans (operates as a bank) then it cannot be a member of the Berne Union (Author interview, US Ex-Im Bank economist, June 16, 2010).

The members of the Berne Union have ten official "guiding principles" including sharing information on activities and cooperating in setting up policies and procedures on export credit and investment insurance.[4] However, there is little in the way of an enforcement mechanism for violators of the principles, and the principles themselves are rather loose guidelines.[5] The main benefit of being a Berne Union member seems to be through the access of information about the business and finance activities of other members. For example, members share information about their activities during the two annual meetings and at various workshops and seminars.[6] During interviews that I conducted in June 2010 with US Ex-Im Bank economists, they stated that subsequent topics to be discussed at the next annual meeting would have likely included whether firms had been having trouble with banks in Greece, in addition to discussing various programs that were initiated by ECAs as a result of the 2008 financial crisis (Author interview, US Ex-Im Bank economist, June 16, 2010). There is also a "Berne Union Intranet" which provides its members and their employees with data and other information about international finance. While many members of the Berne Union are also members of the OECD many are not, and the OECD has strict regulations for its members' extension of export credit facilities.

The OECD is an intergovernmental organization and thus its membership is only comprised of states. While the OECD is also primarily an organization in which higher-income states share and coordinate information on economic and social policies, the OECD also deals with setting guidelines for trade, and more specifically, guidelines for export credit through their Export Credits Division. The first OECD Arrangement designed to restrict or set limits on export credit facilities, formally known as the "Arrangement on Guidelines for Officially Supported Export Credits," came into effect in April 1978 (OECD 1998).[7] Specifically, the Arrangement (or the "Consensus") "is to provide a framework for the orderly use of officially supported export credits" and applies to guidelines for trade-related aid and partially untied aid; including limitations (such as minimum premium benchmarks, minimum cash payments due at or before the starting point of credit, maximum repayment terms and minimum interest rates) on official export credits (OECD 2003: 3).

These restrictions were necessary in order to prevent an export credit subsidy war between the largest developed countries; a race to the bottom based on which country could offer the cheapest interest rates of credit for the export of their goods (Moravcsik 1989: 180–181; Letovsky 1990; Stephens 1999). Moravcsik (1989: 180) explains that these concerns about increased export competition were first discussed in 1973 because leaders believed that the oil and balance of payments crisis in developing countries would make the competition worse. Therefore the Arrangement set minimum rates of interest (7–8 percent) on export credit facilities, minimum payments of the cost of the contract to be borne by the firm (15 percent) and a maximum length of credit (5–10 years) depending on whether the buying country was an OECD country or developing country. This OECD Arrangement "has grown in importance, coverage and scope since its early days" (Stephens 1999: 98). For example, the OECD Arrangement is recognized under the WTO framework. Generally the WTO does not allow governments to subsidize their exports. However, the measures under the Arrangement do not violate WTO rules on subsidies because the WTO Agreement on Subsidies and

Countervailing Measures exempts export credit guarantee schemes if at least 12 original General Agreement on Tariffs and Trade (GATT) members participate in "an international undertaking on official export credits" in order to regulate the use of those guarantees (Felbermayr, Heiland and Yalcin 2012: 4; WTO Agreement on Subsidies and Countervailing Measures, Annex 1, articles j and k). In fact, item (k) in Article 3 of the WTO Agreement on Subsidies and Countervailing Measures gives an exemption for export credits that conform to the specific interest rate provisions of the OECD Arrangement, irrespective of whether the credits are provided by a Participant or non-Participant to the Arrangement (Abel 1998: 15). This means that states that are not Participants in the Arrangement, but are members of the WTO, could legally provide export credits so long as they are within the interest rate provisions of the Arrangement. In 1999, the Arrangement set minimum rates for country credit risk or political risk; prior to this it had only established rates for commercial risk.

One other area in which the Arrangement has evolved over time concerns how countries are assessed for the basis of risk premium categories. Recall that one of the purposes of the first Arrangement was to prevent a subsidy war between (at the time) the five largest economies in their goal to provide exports to developing countries. Even the first Arrangement in 1978 differentiated between terms of credit depending on whether the buying country was developed or developing. This type of classification was further modified to put countries in buyer risk classification categories in order to set minimum standards of lending based on the type of risk. Categories range from 0–7, with only OECD countries in the zero category (no risk) and category 7 indicating the highest risk of nonpayment. Category zero countries are also not supposed to compete with the private financial sector (and generally within each country they do not) but the problem is determining an appropriate level playing field in market conditions between countries (Author interview, US Ex-Im Bank economist, June 16, 2010). The most recent change to the Arrangement in 2010 lowered the minimum premium rates for country credit risk, and set a minimum fee for country and buyer risk for sovereign and non-sovereign lending for countries in the zero category (no risk) (OECD 2010a). Thus, the primary difference between the Exports Credit Division of the OECD and the Berne Union is that rules, requirements, and procedures for regulating the financing of international trade are found in the former whereas in the latter they are understood to be more of an "agreement."

ECA literature

Most of the literature on ECAs has focused on three areas: the initial founding of ECAs, their necessity in order to facilitate some types of foreign export financing, or their general role in facilitating international trade. One of the earliest articles on the founding of the US Ex-Im Bank in 1934 (Pierson 1940: 35–36) details why the US Ex-Im Bank was established (to facilitate trade with the USSR) and, specifically, that Ex-Im was established through Presidential Executive Order to be able to facilitate this type of trade.[8] Pierson (1940: 37) reviews how, not surprisingly, the Ex-Im Bank's policies have changed over time. For example, he notes that in the "early days" loans were made on a "full recourse basis" meaning that the American exporters were obliged to use all of their assets in order to pay the loan; in the same paragraph Pierson describes how this requirement was changed, and that the Bank would underwrite 50 percent to 75 percent of the credit for the loan. This amount has increased over time and currently, Ex-Im will insure up to 85 percent of the credit for the loan; the domestic content of the loan.

Canada's first ECA, the Exports Credits Insurance Corporation founded in 1943, was replaced by the Export Development Corporation (EDC) in 1969 (Baker 2003: 153–154). The EDC operates on a commercial basis so that while technically it is a government agency, it does not operate as Ex-Im does as a "lender of last resort"; which means that Canadian companies often go to the EDC first for trade finance before approaching commercial banks.[9] Much of the financing from the EDC occurs through its "market window" which means that it is a government institution but one that offers "export credit on market terms, enabling them to bypass the OECD Arrangement rules" (US Ex-Im Bank 2009: 57). In 2008, 72 percent of Canada's medium- and long-term transactions took place in this market window (US Ex-Im Bank 2009: 16). There are two reasons that explain why the EDC is more involved in these transactions than US Ex-Im. First, there are fewer Canadian banks (than in the US) available to finance international trade, and second, exports comprise a higher percentage of GDP in the Canadian economy, comprising 43.7 percent of GDP in 2000, compared to 10.7 percent of US GDP in 2000 (Gillespie 2001; Baker 2003: 155). However, the EDC's status as a commercial ECA, and the fact that it operates under a "market window" allowing it to receive government benefits not available to commercial banks (and not following OECD Arrangement rules), has resulted in some disagreement as to whether the EDC operates as a competitive threat (US Ex-Im Bank 2009: 57).[10]

While there is some literature on non-G-7 ECAs, much analysis focuses instead on the G-7 ECAs since as part of the OECD they cooperate on rules and procedures, and are the leading trading countries comprising 34.8 percent of exports and 39.1 percent of imports of world merchandise trade for 2008 (WTO 2009: 12). Letovsky (1990: 34) points out that resources are allocated to export finance in a particular country in proportion to the importance placed on its exports, in addition to the perceived role that the government should play in the economy of the particular state. Thus, Germany's ECA, Hermes (1917), is a private insurance company which acts to support the German government in facilitating export trade financing. Hermes is the most involved in credit insurance and covers losses in Germany, and abroad, with payment terms of up to five years (Baker 2003: 145). France's ECA COFACE (1946) was privatized in 1994 and is also an international leader in export credit insurance, having subsidiaries and employees in over 56 countries around the world (Gianturco 2001: 71). Italy's ECA SACE is controlled by the Italian Ministry of Economy and Finance and insures against political and commercial risks, but with EU states and some members of the OECD, the payments must be deferred for at least 24 months following Arrangement rules.[11] The UK's ECA, the Export Credits Guarantee Division (ECGD) (1919) first operated as government department through parliamentary legislation (Baker 2003).[12] The ECGD is now solely concerned with credit insurance and financing for longer-term commitments, having privatized a section in 1991 to be involved with transactions of less than two years (short-term) Baker (2003: 141).[13] In fact, while European governmental ECAs do not engage in short-term lending, their privatized portions can be involved in short-term transactions of one year or less. The Japanese Bank for International Cooperation (JBIC) works to facilitate both imports (primarily of raw materials to be used for manufactured goods) and exports. The JBIC also explicitly notes that one of its goals is to ensure that Japan has "long-term and stable access" to energy and mineral resources; thus many of the JBICs operations concern financing or loans for infrastructure projects in which the raw materials are supplied back to Japan.[14]

Previous trends in ECA activity

The development and need for ECAs has evolved as the needs for international trade and finance have changed (Beard and Thomas 2006). The early ECAs set up in the 1920s and 1930s were designed to support exports to countries that otherwise would not have occurred primarily due to political risks (e.g. the USSR). While only ECAs from five countries were in existence in 1934 (the UK, France, Italy, Spain and the US), after World War II, the number of ECAs increased as did their competition with each other. These trends were primarily due to the desire of the developed countries to increase their exports to developing countries, and the related benefit of increasing domestic employment (Stephens 1999: 1–2). A general mantra of ECAs is not to compete with private sector financing. In this way governments are indirectly involved in supporting exports and domestic suppliers in order to make up for a "gap" in the marketplace.[15] Thus, the importance of ECA financing would seem to rise and fall depending on the circumstances as to whether there have been "gaps" in the market place. This is a trend that has been evident in previous time periods.

In the early 1970s ECA activity decreased because private sector banks were willing to cover the risks themselves (and to rely on sovereign guarantees) in making loans to developing countries. However, by the late 1970s, as a result of the oil crisis in 1973 and the collapse of commodity prices for many developing countries in the mid 1970s, the governments of these countries began to have serious balance of payments problems, and thus were unable to pay this debt (Gamarra, Pollock and Primo Braga 2009: 13–14). This situation also resulted in many of these countries turning to the Paris Club creditors for debt relief or at least re-structuring of their debt, which will be addressed in Chapter 3. The Paris Club includes official bilateral creditors meaning states and, importantly, institutions of those states especially the ECAs.[16] In some cases, the Paris Club creditors look for comparable relief to be provided by private creditors, suppliers and commercial banks; often referred to as the London Club.[17] However, commercial banks operate differently than government creditors. Due to regulatory policies, commercial banks do not normally reschedule interest payments, something that government creditors will often allow (Bohn 1985: 488). Therefore, one of the problems in the debt crisis of the 1980s was that these countries were defaulting on their loans to private banks which did not have their loans guaranteed by ECAs. Commercial banks then demanded repayment of prior loan obligations, and would not agree to re-finance loans.

This situation is part of a larger discussion about the amount of debt incurred by developing countries, much of it from lending by ECAs. For example, the IMF estimated that more than 24 percent of the indebtedness of developing and transition countries in 1996 was held by ECAs (IMF 1998: 11). The structural adjustment policies set up by the IMF and World Bank were advocated by the Paris Club in order for loan restructuring of a country's external debt. This was important because the

ECAs were still responsible for the small number of loans that they had guaranteed to private banks. Commercial banks also looked for agreements that countries had made with the IMF for assurances that the country was back on track; otherwise known as the "seal of approval."[18]

The commercial, political and exchange rate risks from the debt crisis of the 1980s resulted in increased importance of these types of credit agencies to allow firms to increase their business to the developing and transition economies into the 1990s (Gilman and Wang 2003; Blackmon 2007: 364). This was due to two factors: first, ECA activity to emerging markets, or economies in transition increased markedly as a result of the gap in private financing from commercial banks; second, there was a change in attitude of governments in the 1990s concerning the role that ECAs could play in increasing exports, as described by Kuhn, Horvath and Jarvis:

> many governments, which for a number of years had taken a restrictive stance on export credits, began to pursue export promotion more aggressively, often seeing export promotion as a tool to stimulate economic growth in the recession of the early 1990s.
> (1995: 6–7)

While new commitments of officially supported export credits were roughly $23 billion in 1988, they had increased to almost $70 billion in 1993 (Kuhn et al. 1995: 9). In addition, the largest recipient of export credits for 1993 was Russia and the former USSR, comprising 47.5 percent (up from 16.8 percent in 1987) (ibid). Surprisingly, the ECAs had "continued to incur cash flow deficits" similar to the problems of the 1980s but continued to extend new credits. This situation was dealt with in two ways: first, some debtor countries were making payments on debts previously rescheduled by the Paris Club, providing an income source for agencies; and second, many governments decided to recognize a distinction between old business that was unlikely to be completely recovered (and would have the deficits covered by the relevant government) and new business that would have higher risk assessments (Kuhn et al. 1995: 8–9). Thus, states became more involved in providing finance directly through their ECAs in order to facilitate domestic exports and increase economic growth. Figure 1.1 provides comprehensive data on new commitments of officially supported export credits from 1988–2002.

The data from Figure 1.1 indicate a number of trends. First, there has been a general increase in officially supported export credits from 1988 to 2002 going from about $23 billion in 1988 to $88 billion

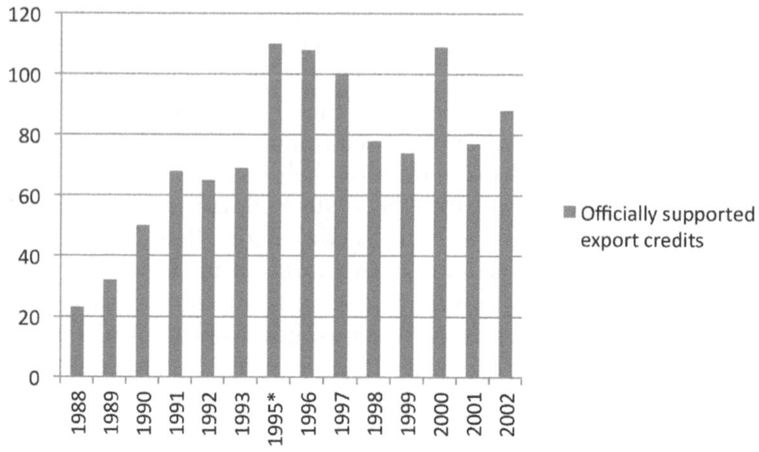

Figure 1.1 Officially supported export credits: new commitments ($bn).

Source: Kuhn et al. 1995: 9; Gilman and Wang 2003: 8.

Note: *Data for 1994 are missing because the data in Kuhn et al. are only through 1993, and the data in Gilman and Wang begin in 1995.

in 2002. Second, the data indicate sharp fluctuations during specific years (1998–2002). Since this data represents only new commitments it is also reflective of economic crises in specific countries such as the Russian crisis in 1998 (reflected in decreases in 1999) and economic crises in Argentina and Brazil (1999–2002) (Gilman and Wang 2003: 10–13). New commitments by ECAs to crisis countries are also explained to be procyclical meaning that the lending goes up when the economy is doing well, and goes down when the economy declines. This is probably also a result of the introduction of higher risk assessments used by some ECAs in the 1990s to try to prevent potential future losses. In the past, new commitments to countries in crisis have fallen during those specific time periods of economic crisis. Chapter 5 will explain how the 2008 crisis resulted in widespread problems with trade finance (resulting in steep trade declines) and higher levels of support from government-supported ECAs.

Conclusion

ECAs have been very prominent in facilitating international trade, especially to developing countries. However, since they often cover risks that the private market deems unacceptable they have supported exports to countries that otherwise would not have qualified for private sector financing due to high risk. Chapter 2 will detail the types of firms that use ECAs as a way to export their goods to developing countries.

Notes

1 ECAs do vary in the percentages of the domestic content of the good that they will finance. For example, the US Ex-Im Bank provides financing for up to 85 percent of the exported good; the domestic content of the good. The exporter is responsible for the other 15 percent although this percentage can be manufactured in the exported country which then provides employment opportunities for the foreign country, of obvious benefit to the foreign government (Author interview, US Ex-Im Bank economist October 3, 2003).

2 There is some debate as to whether private sector insurance is unavailable or just too expensive thereby justifying the need by national exporters for ECAs. In addition, proponents of more laissez-faire economic policy argue that the market failure argument in support of the need for ECAs is wrong and that free markets should be the only determinants of policy. Niskanen (2001: 192) concedes that private credit is often not available in some cases, however, he argues that "[t]he lack of private credit on terms acceptable to a foreign borrower is not an example of market failure but an important signal of the risks of lending to that borrower."

3 The International Credit Insurance Association (ICIA) is not reviewed because its members are private sector companies and they do not all offer export credit insurance. For additional information, see Gianturco 2001: 51–52).

4 http://berneunion.org.uk/guiding-principles.html (June 28, 2010).

5 The website has a disclaimer that the guidelines are not legally binding.

6 http://berneunion.org.uk/guiding-principles.html (June 28, 2010).

7 For a more detailed analysis of the OECD Export Credit Arrangements, see Moravcsik (1989).

8 For an excellent analysis of the history and development of the US Export-Import Bank, see Becker and McClenahan (2003).

9 For additional information on the operations of a commercial ECA, see Gillespie (2001: 230–231).

10 See the chapter by Gillespie, then president of the EDC, in Hufbauer and Rodgriguez in which he defends the EDC and states that the EDC model is not "a competitive threat, but rather an opportunity" (2001: 227).

11 http://sace.it/GruppoSACE/content/en/consumer/products/products_guide/index.html (October 5, 2011). The OECD countries referred to are Australia, Canada, Iceland, Japan, New Zealand, Norway, Switzerland and the US.

12 For a discussion of the initial lending facilities provided by the ECGD, see Buckley 1983: 98–100.

13 Detailed information on the G-7 ECAs is also found in editions of the World's Principle Export Credit Insurance Systems, published by the International Exports Credits Institute.

14 http://jbic.go.jp/en/special/ (September 29, 2010); and detailed in Baker (2003: 151–152).

15 Stephens (1999: 2) uses this phrase and I think it is more appropriate than the concept of market failure to discuss ECAs.
16 http://clubdeparis.org/sections/ (July 14, 2010).
17 The London Club is a very informal group of commercial banks whose representatives (which vary depending on the country in question) meet to discuss restructuring of debts of sovereign borrowers (Stephens 1999: 94).
18 See, for example the discussion in Gamarra et al. (2009: 19–24). The topic of developing country debt being held by ECAs will be addressed in Chapters 2 and 3.

2 Exporting goods to developing countries

In order for global companies to be economically successful they must be able to export their goods. There are at least two interrelated entities that directly or indirectly support firms in this goal. First, the export of goods are generally supported by the domestic government in which they are located. This is because international trade is crucial to the viability of export industries and to the economic viability of most states today (Evans and Oye 2001). Second, national ECAs are set up by governments in order to support exports to international markets by providing guarantees or insurance for the private sector financing of the export contract (Gianturco 2001). Thus, global companies that are involved in international trade rely heavily on the ECAs. One estimate is that the ECAs finance about one out of every eight dollars of world trade (Gianturco 2001: 1). Recall that ECAs often operate to support exports to developing country markets in which commercial bank financing is unavailable or too expensive due to unacceptable political and economic risks that the export contract will not be paid (Stephens 1999).

This chapter will provide evidence to illustrate that support for exports between governments and their national ECAs has resulted in worsening the debt situation of developing countries. To begin with, some of the developing country debt is comprised of loans and guarantees from the ECAs whose activities are largely backed and guaranteed by the governments of those respective agencies (Birdsall, Williamson and Deese 2002: 35; Rieffel 2003: 35). Indeed, in 1999, about 50 percent of the debt of the HIPCs was owed to bilateral creditors (although some was concessional) but almost all of the 13 percent of private creditor debt was also backed by a sovereign guarantee of an ECA (Birdsall, Williamson and Deese 2002: 8). The HIPC countries are a group of countries, most of them in sub-Saharan Africa, identified by the IMF and World Bank as being extremely poor and to be having the most difficulty in improving their external debt situation (Gamarra, Pollock and Primo Braga 2009: 25). High debt is problematic for alleviating poverty in developing countries because debt displaces spending on social services and specifically impacts health spending (Lora and Olivera 2006: 6). Much of this bilateral public sector debt of developing countries is then rescheduled at various time periods through the Paris Club negotiations. The problem is that most of these creditor countries are members of the Paris Club and thus have a "substantial" amount of control over the negotiations of debt that many of their ECAs extended to these debtor countries (Rieffel 2003: 85, 86; Callaghy 2010: 162).

For example, in most debt restructuring arrangements the entire debt stock has been consolidated among the "Paris Club" of creditor countries (Gamarra et al. 2009: 12–13). This debt restructuring process seems to perpetuate the debt cycle for developing countries since after old loans are restructured, they can then be eligible for new export credit loans, under the "subordination strategy." Recall from the introductory chapter that this is the process whereby old loans are subordinated to new credits, allowing many of these countries to be eligible for additional export credit facilities (Kuhn 1994: 24). These types of financing arrangements are an important way that companies, both large and small, are able to export their goods abroad, but it seems that the interests of these firms are superseding what is best for the developing countries.

Official ECAs

As mentioned in Chapter 1, one of the primary ways that firms are able to export their products to developing and transition countries is through trade financing provided by ECAs. In fact, all member states of the OECD have ECAs, in addition to non-member states such as Brazil, Russia, India and China (also known as the BRICs). Governments view the establishment of an ECA as a way to increase their country's exports, which has become even more important in the era of increasing globalized trade. In addition, governments can boast that they are creating jobs through the financing support provided by their ECAs (US Ex-Im Bank 2004 Annual Report: 3). Firms benefit from ECA activity since these financial arrangements allow them to increase their business opportunities to regions that otherwise would have been lost due to unacceptable risk (Blackmon 2011).

ECA financing for developing and transition economies is deemed to be necessary by firms for two reasons. First, while these regions have the greatest potential for increased trade activity, they also entail greater risks of non-payment for exporting firms to do business in those countries. The second reason that ECA financing is necessary is because private sector finance is either unavailable or too expensive especially for medium- or longer-term financing arrangements. Most ECA credit activity has been for medium-term financing for capital goods; and longer-term financing for investment and infrastructure related projects (Kuhn, Horvath and Jarvis 1995: 5, 14). Export industries prefer the ECA insurance because commercial banks covering the risks for these types of projects would charge much higher interest rates. Thus, exporters turn to the ECAs when private sector insurance is either more expensive or not available (Kuhn et al. 1995: 12, 14). Short-term trade credits (two years or less) are seen as less risky, thus they are more often covered by private finance. Short-term credits have also been exempted from debt rescheduling in the past, whereas longer-term debt has been subject to rescheduling (Cline 2005: 20).

Bilateral debt in the context of the Paris Club is defined as "debt between an individual (normally public or sovereign) debtor and a sovereign creditor. Creditors are thus governments or export agencies, and the governments of the debtor countries bear responsibility for repayment of the rescheduled debts" (Stephens 1999: 72). According to the Paris Club website, the category of debt classified as bilateral debt includes "(c)laims granted by States (governments or their appropriate institutions, especially export credit agencies)" (Paris Club 2010). ECAs can be public sector or government entities, or they can be private sector insurers supported by official guarantees. This chapter will focus on public or official debt but it should be kept in mind that if export credits were extended by a private entity, but guaranteed or assumed by a debtor government, that that debt would also qualify for a debt rescheduling agreement (Rieffel 1985: 2; Stephens 1999: 42).

There are a few explanations as to why such little attention is paid to ECAs and to the debt levels that developing and transition countries incur through their activities. First, not much is written about the ECAs and their activity in trade finance in general. Delio Gianturco (2001: 1) begins his book with the statement:

> the "unsung giants" of international finance are the world's export credit agencies (ECAs) – highly specialized financial institutions that currently cover about $800 billion of exports each year but rarely receive the attention of the press or of the average citizen.

Second, and related to the latter point, there is little written about how trade finance is carried out as compared to private financing. Private financing of exports is more common place than official agency trade financing and the former had become more prevalent than public or government financing for developing countries, especially during the 1990s when private finance was abundant (Borensztein, Yeyati and Panizza 2006: 112). The following section provides an overview of the breakdown of debt by creditor from lower-middle income countries in order to illustrate the amount of debt held by ECAs.

The World Bank classifies total external debt stocks as the sum of public and publicly guaranteed debt; private non-guaranteed long-term debt; short-term debt and the use of IMF credit (Global Development Finance database). For the lower-middle income countries ($1,006 to $3,975 Gross National Income (GNI) per capita), high levels of external debt are comprised of public and publicly guaranteed debt which is defined as, "long-term external obligations of public debtors, including the national government, political subdivisions (or an agency of either), and autonomous public bodies, and external obligations of private debtors that are guaranteed for repayment by a public entity." This debt indicator comprises some of the debt owed to public ECAs because it includes debt from the national government and the private debt that is guaranteed for repayment. This debt indicator is also the highest for the years 1980–2010 (in five-year intervals) when compared to bilateral concessional, multilateral and multilateral concessional for the same time frame (Global Development Finance database). The total external debt stocks for these countries using the previous data range was $3.6 trillion; the composition of public and publicly guaranteed debt was $2.4 trillion comprising almost 67 percent of total external debt stocks (Global Development Finance database). In addition, for this group of countries this debt indicator is much larger than the debt that is comprised of private nonguaranteed long-term debt ($654 billion; about 17 percent of total external debt stocks) defined as, "long-term external obligations of private debtors that are not guaranteed for repayment by a public entity." In other words, debt held by private creditors (banks) that is long term and not guaranteed by an ECA. The composition of short-term debt defined as, "debt that has an original maturity of one year or less. Available data permit no distinction between public and private nonguaranteed short-term debt." If the short-term debt is public, then it would be guaranteed by an ECA.

While there is no distinct debt indicator representing loans from official ECAs, the previous data illustrate that debt levels comprised of ECAs have represented a substantial part of the debt of developing economies. The following section details how global companies use ECAs to help them with their exports. The section will also illustrate how ECAs are involved in the extension of export credits to developing countries, how this debt is then rescheduled through the Paris Club, followed by the extension of new export credits from the ECAs.

Firms that use ECAs

Complete publicly available data on ECAs is extremely difficult to find. One US Ex-Im Bank official explained that European ECAs (Germany, France, Italy) want a high level of secrecy about their data and therefore make very few public documents available (Author interview, Ex-Im Bank official, May 7, 2012). Non-OECD ECAs operate with an even higher level of secrecy and they do not have to follow certain "Arrangement" rules on officially supported export credits since they are not part of the OECD (Blackmon 2012; Moravcsik 1989). The US Ex-Im Bank is set up differently in this aspect, in that as part of its charter, it is mandated to submit a report on the competitiveness of its export financing services annually to Congress (US Ex-Im Bank Competitiveness Reports, any year, introductory material). The ECAs of the UK (the ECGD) and Canada (EDC) provide some comparable firm level data, but much of the detailed data on business activity supported by ECAs contained in the US Ex-Im Bank Competitiveness Reports is not found in other ECA reports.

The US Ex-Im Bank also publishes Annual Reports that include data on virtually all of their activities. For example, there is data on the types of authorizations by market (country) and the amount of loans, guarantees and insurance or exposure to each country. For each fiscal year, if a country receives new loans or new long-term guarantees, the amount is provided as well as information on the obligor, guarantor and principal supplier (the firm) for the project. There is also information on "Paris Club Bilateral Agreements" including countries to which debt relief and/or debt rescheduling was provided. In Fiscal Year (FY) 2004, the US Ex-Im Bank provided debt relief and/or debt rescheduling to 15 countries; in FY 2003 debt relief and/or debt rescheduling was provided to 13 countries (US Ex-Im Bank 2004 Annual Report: 42). Countries that had debt rescheduled in FY 2003 included Coite d'Ivoire ($26,715), DRC (Zaire) ($597,227), Indonesia ($259,329), Macedonia ($10,523), Pakistan ($220,053) and Yugoslavia ($274,014). Four of those six countries DRC (Zaire),

Indonesia, Pakistan and Yugoslavia also had debt rescheduled in FY 2004 (US Ex-Im Bank 2004 Annual Report: 42).

However, what is surprising is that some of the countries that had debt rescheduled in FY 2003 or FY 2004 also had new long-term guarantees, or new loans in FY 2004 and in 2005 from the US Ex-Im Bank. Loan guarantees basically guarantee to the private lender that the Ex-Im Bank will pay the lender the outstanding principal and interest on the loan if the borrower defaults (US Ex-Im Bank 2004 Annual Report: 35). This type of guarantee from an official creditor-country agency also means that the credit would be dealt with through Paris Club negotiations (Rieffel 1985: 2). This is problematic for these countries because it sets up a revolving door of rescheduled debt, new debt and rescheduled debt again.

For example, Nigeria had $915,934 in debt rescheduled in FY 2004, yet benefitted from a long-term guarantee in FY 2004 of over $18 million in order for Nortel Networks Inc. to provide Bourdex Telecommunications with telecommunications equipment (US Ex-Im Bank 2004 Annual Report: 31). Nigeria also benefitted from a long-term guarantee in FY 2005 of $13,488 in order for HSBC Bank PLC to authorize a credit increase for equipment supply and installation (US Ex-Im Bank 2005 Annual Report: 31).[1] Pakistan had $220,053 in debt rescheduled in FY 2003, yet benefitted from a long-term guarantee in FY 2004 of $3,772,737, in order to buy commercial aircraft from The Boeing Co.; Pakistan subsequently had $2,413 in debt rescheduled that same year (US Ex-Im Bank 2004 Annual Report: 42). Quiport, a firm in Ecuador, was provided a loan for $70 million from the US Ex-Im Bank so that the firm could have Caterpillar Inc. construct a new international airport in FY 2004 (US Ex-Im Bank 2004 Annual Report: 28). Ecuador then had $2,591 debt rescheduled under Paris Club Bilateral Agreements in FY 2005 (US Ex-Im Bank 2005 Annual Report: 42). New export credits, or even loans in one case, are being extended by the US Ex-Im Bank seemingly without regard to the financial difficulties that these countries are having in paying off these debts. Global companies certainly seem to be benefitting from these export contracts, especially if it is the case that these exports would have been otherwise forgone without the US Ex-Im Bank financing. The following section will explain the terms of the export contract between US companies and the US Ex-Im Bank.

The listing of principal suppliers or firms in the Ex-Im Bank publications includes large multinational firms such as Boeing, General Electric, General Motors, Nortel Lucent Technologies, Caterpillar,

Motorola Inc. and ABB Lummus Global. These represent very large well-funded multinational firms although in its mandate the US Ex-Im Bank is only authorized to support US exports and/or providing funding to foreign entities in order for them to purchase US exports. There are various reasons as to why US firms use Ex-Im Bank financing. It is likely that for many firms the high cost of private sector finance may make the export deal not worth the expense. Indeed, in a series of interviews that I conducted in 2003 with US business representatives that used US Ex-Im Bank financing for exports to two former Soviet Union republics, they stated categorically that Ex-Im Bank financing was the deciding factor in whether or not the business transaction would be concluded (Blackmon 2011: 84–88). That is not to say that the country risk criteria was not factored into the business decision in some cases, but representatives were aware that the Ex-Im Bank conducts its own risk analysis and it was presumed that if the Ex-Im Bank were willing to guarantee the financing then the risks were acceptable. This is important because the US Ex-Im Bank will only provide guarantees or insurance for up to 85 percent of a privately financed loan contract; the firm has to supply 15 percent of the contract up front (Blackmon 2011: 86).

The 85 percent is also referred to as the domestic content of the export contract (the percentage that is manufactured in the US). This means that the firm can have the remaining portion of the export contract assembled or manufactured in the importing country; which can include painting equipment, assembling additional parts etc. This option of having some of the assembly done in the importing country is attractive to the host government because it allows for employment of local workers, training programs and certification of factories for parts assembly (Blackmon 2011: 86). By dollar value, large firms have received the most support from the US Ex-Im Bank, however smaller firms have benefitted from a higher number of transactions from the US Ex-Im Bank (Ilias 2012: 2). The following section provides information on firms supported by other ECAs.

The UK's ECA the Export Credits Guarantee Department (ECGD) participated in nine Paris Club agreements to reschedule debt in 2004–2005: Iraq, Nicaragua, Niger, Ethiopia, Senegal, Ghana, Madagascar and Congo Republic (all but Iraq are HIPC countries) and Gabon (ECGD 2004–2005: 15). This section in the Annual Report notes that if the HIPC countries follow the HIPC Initiative and successfully reach the Completion Point, that they are no longer required to service their debts to ECGD, and that the debt is irrevocably written-off. Per ECGD policy, "(a)s long as they (the countries) remain on track with their IMF/World Bank supported programmes, the UK will agree to forgiveness of all their debt and the Department for International Development will pay ECGD on their behalf" (ECGD Annual Report 2004–2005: 15). However, one of the primary criticisms of the HIPC Initiative is that the HIPC countries were unlikely to be able to ever pay off this debt, and furthermore, that not much new money would then be directed toward poverty alleviating initiatives (Cohen 2001; Easterly 2001; Chauvin and Kraay 2005). Thus, in these cases, the debt is forgiven but there are no new resources directed at alleviating poverty from the debt owed to ECGD.

The list of exporters to which guarantees were issued by ECGD included large firms such as Airbus SAS (by far the firm that received the highest level of support), Capital Valves Ltd., Kellogg Brown & Root Ltd., Rolls-Royce Plc., Motorola Ltd. and Guralp Systems Ltd. (ECGD Annual Report 2004–2005: 16–17). Two other European Union (EU) ECAs, France (COFACE) and Germany (Euler Hermes) also participate in support for Airbus and for other transactions. One specific transaction explained that ECGD, COFACE and Euler Hermes "cooperated with commercial lenders to support purchases of Global Standard for Mobile Communications for mobile phone equipment" from those three countries (the UK, France and Germany) by Pakistan Mobile Communications Ltd. The UK's portion of this transaction was stated to be $50 million (ECGD Annual Report 2004–2005: 23).

In 2005–2006 the ECGD participated in Paris Club agreements to reschedule debt with Zambia, Indonesia and Nigeria. Zambia received its final debt treatment under HIPC, meaning that all remaining debt was forgiven. It was also noted that Indonesian payments under the current bilateral debt agreements due in 2005 were deferred in order to provide relief from the 2004 Tsunami (ECGD Annual Report 2005–2006: 15). However, this same document reported that Indonesia was also issued a guarantee for £4.6 million in support of exports from Greys Exports Ltd. for an EODD System and Equipment Project (ECGD Annual Report 2005–2006: 16). In a subsequent ECGD Annual Report (2007–2008: 12) Indonesia was also issued a guarantee for £1.6 million in support of exports from Fernau Avionics Ltd. for the purchase of radar equipment.

Ghana was previously involved in a Paris Club rescheduling in 2004–2005 with ECGD; however, in 2008–2009 the country was issued a guarantee for £18.7 million in support of exports from PW Ltd. to support the Kotoka International Airport Extension (ECGD Annual Report 2008–2009: 12). In addition, Nigeria made its final payment to ECGD on April 26, 2006 per its agreement with its Paris Club creditors. Nigeria does not qualify for the HIPC Initiative since it is not an International Development Association (IDA) only country, having previously been provided loans from the International Bank for Reconstruction and Development (IBRD). An argument has also been made that Nigeria (as an oil rich member of Organization of the Petroleum Exporting Countries (OPEC)) should not need the assistance of HIPC (Callaghy 2010: 173–177). However, ECGD or, more correctly, UK companies working with ECGD, wasted no time in working out three new export contracts with Nigeria to be guaranteed by ECGD. First, Airbus SAS secured a guarantee and/or insurance policy (the table did not differentiate between the two) for £30.4 million, and Gentec Energy Plc. secured two separate guarantees and/or insurance policies for a total of £21 million for gas-capture power plants (ECGD Annual Report 2008–2009: 12).

These examples have illustrated that export credits are being extended by the UK's ECGD to countries having previously requested debt rescheduling under a Paris Club agreement. It should be noted that these cases do have more of a time lag between Paris Club agreements and the extension of new export credits than did some of the cases with US Ex-Im Bank financing. As of June 2012, neither Ghana nor Nigeria had requested debt rescheduling from the Paris Club. However, both countries are still classified by the World Bank as lower-middle income economies (as of 2012) and it is important to question whether the continued extension of these export credits, which add to the debt levels of these countries, is an appropriate method to move these countries forward in their socio-economic development. The following section provides information on the Boeing Company and Airbus as the two of the biggest beneficiaries of ECA supported financing from the US Ex-Im Bank and the UK's ECGD, France's COFACE and Germany's Euler Hermes.

The Boeing Company was one of the "featured companies" profiled in the 2005 Ex-Im Annual Report, which explained, "(b)oeing is one of the leading exporters in the US . . . and that in FY 2005, Ex-Im Bank helped to finance the export of 78 Boeing aircraft to 19 different airlines in 18 different countries" (US Ex-Im Bank 2005 Annual Report: 13). The firm profile also noted that the competition that Boeing faces in the international market from Airbus and its financing support from the ECAs of the UK, Germany and France and that "(b)y guaranteeing the loans of commercial banks to foreign-based airlines that purchase or lease Boeing aircraft, Ex-Im Bank 'levels the playing field'" in its competition with Airbus as the only two manufacturers of large commercial aircraft in the world (ibid., quotes in original).

Information from the ECGD on its support for Airbus is also detailed in various reports. The 2005–2006 ECGD Annual Report noted that the value of guarantees issued by Airbus deliveries increased to 44 percent of business issued (the previous percentage level was not provided) which was explained to be a "significant" part of ECGD export support (ECGD 2005–2006 Annual Report: 6). The 2008–2009 ECGD Annual Report noted that the value of guarantees comprised of Airbus deliveries increased to 72 percent of the business underwritten by ECGD and export credit support from France, Germany and the UK was reported to account for 21 percent of the total deliveries of Airbus for 2008–2009 (ECGD 2008–2009 Annual Report: 8). The following section examines how global companies use Canada's export agency.

Canada's ECA, the Export Development Corporation (EDC) operates a little differently in that it both helps Canadian firms export abroad, and it provides financing to Canadian firms that may not necessarily be exporting abroad. For example, in December 2009, EDC provided $Cdn.5–15 million in financing to the Canadian firm Motovan Corporation for the "Sale of various Canadian goods and services" in which the country of transaction was listed as Canada (Individual Transaction Information https://19.edc.ca/edcsecure/disclosure/DisclosureView.aspx?yr=2009&lang=EN). In this and other examples, EDC was guaranteeing payment to the firm, Motovan Corporation. So EDC acts more as a commercial yet public ECA although it is not privatized like COFACE and Euler Hermes. Canadian exports comprise one of the highest levels of Gross Domestic Product (GDP) of all the countries in the OECD, yet there are few banks that focus on the trade financing needs of Canadian companies; the EDC performs this task exclusively (Gillespie 2001: 228–229).

The firms that the EDC assists in exporting abroad include Yamana Gold Inc. providing financing in the amount of $Cdn.50–100 million in December 2009 to Brazil for "General Corporate Purposes"; MacDonald, Dettwiler and Associates Ltd. provided financing in the amount of $Cdn.250–500 million to Ukraine for the sale of satellite equipment to Ukraine State Enterprise (Individual Transaction Information https://19.edc.ca/edcsecure/disclosure/DisclosureView.aspx?yr=2009&lang=EN).

The information provided by the EDC also illustrates the way that global firms can use ECAs to their advantage based on their transnational status. Or more specifically, that they can take advantage of using

ECAs in several host countries in order to support their export activity. For example, Nortel Networks Limited had two separate transactions in December 2009 for financing from the EDC for the sale of telecommunications equipment to India; one transaction in the amount of \$Cdn.5–15 million, and the other in the amount of \$Cdn.15–25 million. Nortel Networks had previously benefitted from long-term guarantees from the US Ex-Im Bank for the sale of telecommunications equipment to Nigeria. Ford Motor Company of Canada, Limited was also able to benefit from financing from EDC for the "support for future procurement of various Canadian goods and services" in the amount of \$Cdn.100–250 million to "various countries" (Individual Transaction

Table 2.1 Global companies supported by ECAs

Country of ECA	*Company*	*Industry classification*	*Sales \$mn*	*Employees*
Canada	Nortel Networks Ltd.	Telecommunications	620.00	30,329
Canada	Motovan Corporation	Motor vehicle parts	81.75	150
Canada	Yamana Gold Inc.	Gold ore/silver ore mining	2,106.00	N/A
Canada	Mac Donald, Dettwiler and Associates Ltd.	Applications software	45.69	305
Canada	Ford Motor Company of Canada Ltd.	Passenger cars	2,780.00	13,200
France	Airbus Sas (only for France listed as "Sas")	Civilian aircraft	38,763.00	5,709
UK	Capital Valves Ltd.	Machinery/ industrial goods	28.75	11
UK	Kellogg Brown & Root Ltd.	Technical services	1,328.96	1,164
UK	Rolls Royce Plc.	Motor vehicle parts	16.70	950
UK	Motorola Solutions Ltd.	Telecommunications equipment	877.17	1,471
UK	Guralp Systems Ltd.	Measuring/precision instruments	14.95	85
UK	Gentec Energy Plc.	Engines/turbines	51.16	19
US	Nortel Networks Inc.	Telecommunications equipment	0.28	4
US	Boeing Industry	Civilian aircraft	68,735.00	171,700
US	Caterpillar Inc.	Construction machinery	60,138.00	125,099
US	General Electric	Diversified holding companies	142,237.00	301,000

Source: Factiva Powered by Dow Jones Companies database; accessed May 17, 2012.

Information https://19.edc.ca/edcsecure/disclosure/DisclosureView.aspx?yr=2009&lang=EN). There is a problem in deciphering the country of transaction for some of the data from the EDC in that it is not complete data. Table 2.1 shows specific information on the global companies that have been profiled in this chapter, including their industry classification and their size (represented by sales and number of employees).

Many of these firms had multiple company names or subsidiaries in many different countries, and some very large firms had many subsidiaries in the same country. For example, the Boeing Company with one location in the US and an industry classification of "civil aircraft" was the information used in Table 2.1, however "Boeing Aerospace Operations Inc." also had a location in the US but with an industry classification of "technical services" which was not used because the descriptive information provided for Boeing was for aircraft in the 2005 US Ex-Im Bank Annual Report. Therefore, in searching the Factiva database, I matched the industry classification with the project description listed in the report of the corresponding ECA. Boeing also had listings in Australia, Ireland and Canada, just to name a few (Factiva database Powered by Dow Jones Companies, accessed May 17, 2012). The previous information shows that global firms have used ECA financing in order to be able to export their goods to developing and/or lower-middle income countries.

Conclusion

Global companies use ECAs in a variety of ways to support the export of their goods abroad. The problems with this scenario arise when the export of goods are to developing countries that already have high levels of debt. The primacy of the interests of the entities supporting these exports is most visible when some of the developing country debt is owed to an ECA. Global companies (through their national ECAs) are able to continue exporting their goods to these countries, sales that otherwise would have been lost due to the lack of private sector finance. However, these export credits or loans could possibly need to be rescheduled in the future, thereby perpetuating this debt cycle. Chapter 3 will illustrate these problems by examining the development of the HIPC program and more specifically how the debt relief provided under the HIPC was in large part due to Paris Club debt. In addition, Chapter 3 will provide evidence to show how the debt owed to the ECAs is a troubling factor in the longer-term debt problems of some developing countries.

Note

1 These tables do not provide data on the obligor or guarantor so it is not clear whether they were made under the sovereign (to a government) or commercial risk category. Since they are guaranteed by an official agency, and are long term they can be rescheduled under Paris Club Agreements (Rieffel 1985: 19).

3 Paris Club debt rescheduling and the HIPC Initiative

Since the mid 1950s, bilateral, private and commercial creditors have agreed, during various time periods, to reschedule and restructure debt from debtor countries in order to prevent default and to allow these countries to fix their economic problems. These previous arrangements were beneficial for the middle-income countries, but were not successful in easing debt burdens or in improving economic growth in the poorest or low-income countries, especially those in sub-Saharan Africa (Gamarra, Pollock and Braga 2009: 25). As a result of increasing external debt difficulties in low-income countries, the HIPC Initiative would be offered to low-income countries that agreed to follow IMF and World Bank supported programs of economic reform and adjustment. It is important to explain why the IMF and World Bank implemented these fundamental policy changes.

Decision-making in the institutions

Neoliberal institutionalists essentially believe that international institutions serve the interests of states by fostering cooperation through shared interests (Mitrany 1975; Keohane 1984). Keohane (1984: 9) extends this framework by pointing out that in some instances cooperation can develop "on the basis of complementary interests, and that institutions, broadly defined, affect the patterns of cooperation that emerge." States, especially powerful ones like the US, are important decision makers in the institutions. Studies have found that the influence of the US is a determining factor in explaining changes in the institutions since the US is one of the largest shareholders in the IMF and the Bank (Thacker 1999; Woods 2003; 2006). While the voting and decision-making processes are somewhat different between the Fund and the Bank, the US has "veto power" over substantial policy changes in the Fund due to the voting rules and the percentage of votes that the US holds on the Executive Board. The US is the largest shareholder in the Fund with about 17 percent of the total quotas, while the country with the next largest quota is Japan with 6.3 percent.[1] The US percentage is important because substantial policy changes in the Fund require a majority of at least 85 percent of votes, which effectively means that US support would be required to reach the 85 percent threshold (Woods 2003: 98–99).

External factors

Non-governmental organizations (NGOs) have also been focusing on powerful states in order to affect change in the institutions. NGOs have increased markedly since the end of the Cold War and are having a greater degree of influence over international politics, including attempts to shape the policies of states and by extension, intergovernmental organizations (Cleary 1995; Matthews 1997; O'Brien et al. 2000; Blackmon 2009). The influence of the US also impacts the institutions indirectly through the lobbying efforts of NGOs in a number of ways. First, most of the larger well funded NGOs have offices in Washington DC and thus have access to the US Congress which becomes important when US funding for the institutions is to be discussed (Weaver and Leiteritz 2005: 372–373; Williams 1999: 235–236). Woods (2003: 112) explains that NGOs will focus on the US in order to affect change at the institutions because

> the United States is, among states, the most powerful to demand change. In particular, NGOs turn to the US Congress because it has the power – and uses it – to impose conditions on any approval given for the replenishment of the IDA in the World Bank or any increase in IMF quotas.

Busby's (2007) study found that the efforts of the Jubilee 2000 campaign in securing debt relief for the poorest countries were in fact crucial for the enhancements to the HIPC Initiative (explained below). Furthermore, his research focused on the importance for NGOs (and individuals) to identify the "policy gatekeepers" that were crucial to the decision-making and policy-making processes in order to garner the support of the US for debt relief (Busby 2007: 266–269). Busby (2007: 271) concludes that:

> One central finding is that policy gatekeepers are prepared to invest significant, albeit limited, amounts of resources to support norms-based policies when advocates have tapped into values that have broader societal appeal.

NGOs are working through states to get policies changed at the institutions; but states as well as the institutions benefit from this mutual cooperation.

Internal factors

Internal factors also explain why the institutions were willing to change their policies. Vaubel (1991, 1996) points to institutional principle-agent problems with the IMF in that their staff operates similarly to staff in other bureaucracies in trying to prove (and support) their reasons for existence.[2] Since the previous Structural Adjustment Policies advocated by the institutions resulted in increasing poverty in the countries that implemented them (most notably in Africa) a different approach to poverty alleviation would have been welcomed from the standpoint of the survival of the institutions. Additionally, the "Fifty Years is Enough" campaign, coupled with increasing demonstrations at IMF and World Bank annual meetings, would result in a renewed focus to change the internal mandates of the institutions to involve the participation of poor countries in development strategies (Stiglitz 2002: 50).

The enhanced HIPC

In 1999, the IMF and World Bank launched a comprehensive review through a public consultative process of the HIPC and concluded that while the HIPC was a positive step toward dealing with unsustainable debt, the criteria of the Initiative should be modified in order to allow more countries to qualify for assistance. Specific changes undertaken to enhance the HIPC included the lowering of targets and thresholds (of debt-to-export ratios), shortening the performance criteria (thereby accelerating the delivery of debt relief) and strengthening the link between debt relief and poverty reduction (Andrews, Boote, Rizavi and Singh 1999: 11–13). This last change would specifically link debt relief to social development and poverty reduction through country-designed reforms detailed in the preparation of a Poverty Reduction Strategy Paper (PRSP). The enhanced HIPC Initiative was designed to free up governmental financial resources that had previously gone to servicing a country's multilateral debt and re-direct these resources for use in specific poverty reduction programs as outlined by the PRSP (IMF and World Bank, 2001; Gupta et al. 2004; IMF Independent Evaluation Office (IEO) 2004).[3] However, countries must meet certain criteria in order to be considered for the HIPC Initiative. First, the HIPC Initiative limits country eligibility to those low-income countries authorized to borrow through the International Development Association (IDA) arm of the World Bank and the Enhanced Structural Adjustment Facility (ESAF) of the IMF.[4] Second, countries are required to be under a structural adjustment program supported by the IMF and World Bank, and they receive concessional financing from the institutions during this time period. Support is also provided from the Paris Club creditors who offer countries flow-reschedulings on Naples terms (67 percent Net Present Value (NPV) reduction) during this initial stage, also known as the "pre-decision point."

After establishing a successful track record for three years under the adjustment program and the rescheduling agreements, a country reaches the "decision point" whereby the IMF and World Bank conduct a debt sustainability analysis to determine whether the previous debt-relief mechanisms would be sufficient for the country to reach external debt sustainability or whether further assistance would be required under the Initiative (Andrews et al. 1999: 4–5; Blackmon 2010). If a country qualifies for assistance, it moves onto the second (or interim) stage during which the country continues to implement the IMF/WB adjustment program with concessional lending and the Paris Club creditors provide flow-reschedulings on Lyon terms (up to 80 percent NPV reduction). At this stage, countries receive comparable treatment from the non-Paris Club bilateral creditors, commercial creditors and they receive relief from debt service falling due from the IMF and World Bank. Countries are also required to implement a PRSP at this stage. As long as the country continues to implement the IMF/WB program "satisfactorily" the Paris Club creditors agree to provide stock-of-debt operation on Lyon terms when the country reaches the "completion point." This process is depicted in Figure 3.1.

In fact, indebted countries have an incentive just to *request* entrance into the E-HIPC process, since even at the first stage, they qualify for flow rescheduling on Naples terms. If the IMF and World Bank determine that this "pre-decision point" treatment is enough for the country to reach sustainability measures, then the country is not eligible for assistance under E-HIPC (see Figure 3.1). As long as the qualifying

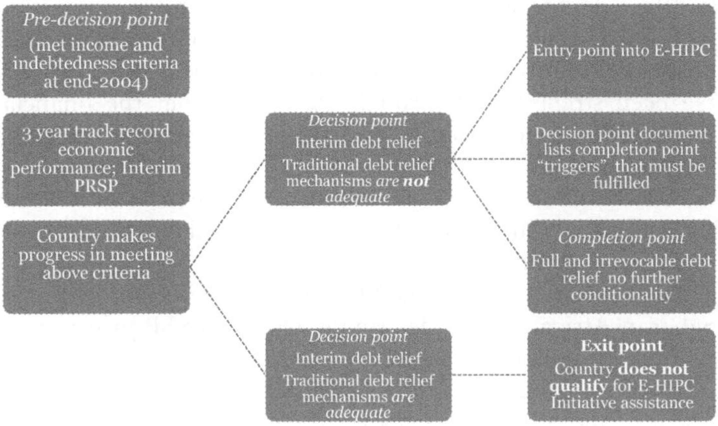

Figure 3.1 The E-HIPC process.

qualifying country makes adequate process, and reaches the completion point, the country will benefit from flow-rescheduling under Lyon terms (up to 80 percent NPV reduction). In addition, there is some evidence that countries reaching the completion point see better results in poverty alleviation compared with countries that have not, in measures such as reductions in infant mortality and decreases in the poverty gap (Apodaca and Blackmon 2016).

Previous studies of the HIPC Initiative

There is a substantial body of literature that is generally critical of these new initiatives by the IMF and World Bank, primarily based on the assumption that the policies are the still the same, and that the only change is a shift in language to a framework referring to a new form of "governance" (Grindle 2004; Weber 2004; Weaver and Leiteritz 2005). Imboela's (2005) study examined the 2002 PRSP of Zambia and concluded that it was not fundamentally different from previous policies of the financial institutions, and that it did not represent a new approach to understanding poverty in Zambia. More focused research on the PRSPs has concentrated on the early processes of preparation and collaboration on the PRSPs, by examining whether the process has in fact included involvement by the governments, civil society groups and other NGOs. Stewart and Wang (2006: 291) provide a comprehensive analysis of all of the PRSPs produced since 1999 and examine, "the extent to which they have increased national ownership or programmes and thereby have empowered the countries" instead of the financial institutions. They conclude that while civil society groups may have been strengthened through the PRSPs, that the financial institutions still have more control over the process of developing the PRSPs (Stewart and Wang 2006: 316–318). Holtom (2007: 247) finds strengths and weaknesses in the development of Tanzania's PRSP but notes that civil society involvement was strengthened overall throughout the formation of the PRSP.

The purpose of one study of the PRSP processes in eight countries in sub-Saharan Africa, was to determine whether PRSP *processes* of poverty reduction policies were in fact "leading to poverty reduction plans" in topics including attitudes, institutional changes and the development of monitoring systems for the countries studied (Booth 2003: 133). While the study did not analyze PRSP documents or engage in content analysis of the specific strategies followed by the countries, the research resulted in some important initial findings about the PRSP process. First, the study found that the process of preparing the PRSP could lead to more effective poverty reduction, although the experiences of the countries varied (Booth 2003: 131, 140). Second, the study found that the issue of poverty in the countries, along with the concerns of the poor have been addressed to a wider degree. Although, defining goals and priorities to address these issues were not clear (Booth 2003: 147–148). Third, that additional progress was needed in the performance assessment mechanisms used by all actors involved, and that they should be better coordinated to the specific criteria outlined in the PRSPs (Booth, 2003: 153).

An additional study on the design of initial PRSPs examined whether civil society organizations had been adequately involved in the participatory process of developing the PRSPs (McGee, Levene and Hughes 2002).[5] The study concluded that, overall, civil society participation was a positive addition to the process, but that countries would benefit from greater participation from these groups. Regarding the PRSPs impacts on poverty, the authors stated that, "civil society participation in PRSP processes in all countries (lead) to a broadening and diversification of the actors who engage in poverty discourse and the policy process" (McGee, Levene and Hughes 2002: viii). This represents an important step in one of the specific purposes of the PRSP, which was to focus the efforts of all actors toward poverty reduction.

The HIPC Initiative was designed around the premise that low-income countries could alleviate poverty if they spent less money servicing their debt and instead re-directed this money toward programs involving social services (Gupta, Clements, Guin-Siu and Leruth 2004; Blackmon 2008, 2010). One of the primary arguments against providing debt relief is that this will create a "moral hazard" situation in that countries will borrow recklessly believing that their debts will eventually be forgiven (Easterly 2001: 24). Indeed, Easterly (2001, 2002) has been highly critical of the HIPC debt relief proposal, including the fact that many of these countries became heavily indebted after previous private and bilateral debt relief initiatives. Other scholars such as Stiglitz (2007: 226, 231) and Sachs (1989: 280–281) have been more supportive of the HIPC Initiative, arguing that debt relief is needed for the poorest countries to be able to provide for their citizens and for the countries to get out of poverty. Jeffrey Sachs (2006: vii) states emphatically, "(I) took up the cause of debt cancellation as opposed to debt servicing, arguing that both creditor and debtor interests would be improved by canceling a mountain of unpayable debt."

Debt forgiveness was viewed as necessary for the HIPC countries for many reasons. First, studies have shown that large debt levels reduce spending on social expenditures. Borensztein, Yeyati and Panizza (2006) argue that "excessive" levels of debt have curtailed spending available for poverty-alleviating expenditures. Second, poverty alleviation as an international societal problem has been recognized by many organizations that supported debt forgiveness. Non-governmental organizations including Oxfam and the Jubliee 2000 movement were instrumental in framing the "broader societal appeal" of debt relief for the poorest countries (Cohen 2001). These organizations also helped to build support for debt relief in the US and the UK (Busby 2007). The importance placed on the development of strategies to alleviate poverty was recognized by the UN Millennium Declaration and was included as part of the Millennium Development Goals (MDGs). In fact, Goal 8 of the MDGs includes the E-HIPC initiative as part of addressing the needs of the least developed countries in order to facilitate development as a global partnership (United Nations Development Program (UNDP) 2004).

However, the high level of public and publicly guaranteed debt comprised of debt owed to the Paris Club creditors has received much less attention as contributing to the indebtedness problems of developing countries. For example, while debt owed to the multilaterals comprised only 25 percent of all developing country debt by 1999, publicly guaranteed commercial debt comprised 42 percent of all developing country debt by 1999 (Birdsall et al. 2002: 4–25). In fact, much of the literature on developing country debt does not analyze debt incurred as a result of ECA activity (Easterly 2002; Bird and Milne 2003; Gunter 2011).[6] This is surprising because public or governmental ECAs primarily function as tools by which states are able to facilitate the export of domestic goods to developing and transition economies (Stephens 1999). According to a recent study by Eurodad, almost 80 percent of poor countries' debts to European governments came from export credits, and not from development loans (Eurodad 2011). An analysis of export credits provided by the ECAs is crucial for understanding how developing countries have been able to incur such large debt levels.

The composition of the external debt of lower-middle income developing countries

As mentioned in Chapter 2, the World Bank classifies total external debt stocks as the sum of: public and publicly guaranteed debt (PPG), private non-guaranteed long term debt (PNG), the use of IMF credit and short term debt (Global Development Finance database). The World Bank defines public and publicly guaranteed debt as, "long-term external obligations of public debtors, including the national government, political subdivisions (or an agency of either), and autonomous public bodies, and external obligations of private debtors that are guaranteed for repayment by a public entity."[7] Also recall that this debt indicator comprises some of the debt owed to public ECAs because it includes debt from the national government and private debt that is guaranteed for repayment. Private nonguaranteed long-term debt is defined as, "long-term external obligations of private debtors that are not guaranteed for repayment by a public entity." In other words, debt held by private creditors (banks) that is long term and not guaranteed by an ECA. The composition of short-term debt (public and private) is defined as debt having an original maturity of one year or less. Specific amounts of these individual categories of debt for lower-middle income countries are presented in rows one through five in Figure 3.2.[8]

Public and Publically Guaranteed (PPG) Bilateral Debt and Public and Publically Guaranteed (PPG) Bilateral Concessional Debt (presented in rows six and seven in Figure 3.2) are indicators that are not included in the sum of external debt stocks as used by the Bank. However, they are used in this data analysis because they are important both as comparisons to the levels of different types of debt these

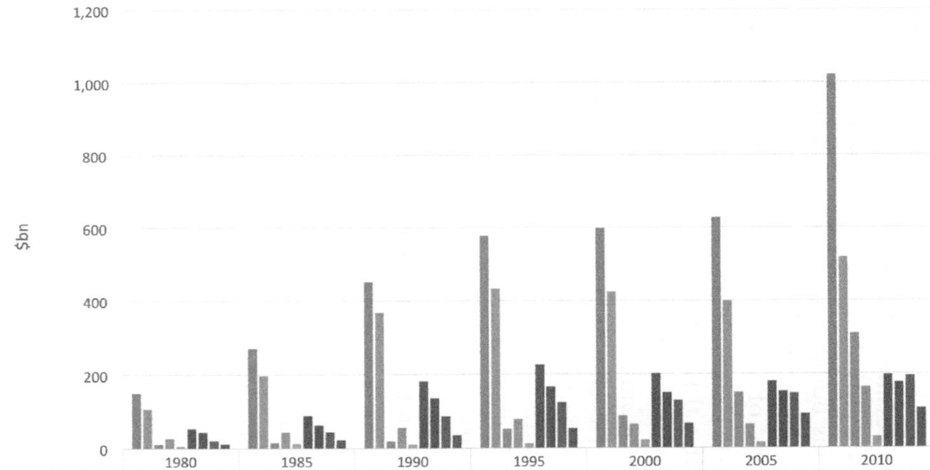

	1980	1985	1990	1995	2000	2005	2010
External debt stocks, total (current US$)	150	269.7	453.6	577.8	598.5	628.6	1021
External debt stocks, public and publicly guaranteed (PPG) (current US$)	106.2	197.6	367.5	434.4	424.5	399	518.3
External debt stocks, private nonguaranteed (PNG) (current US$)	11.1	15.4	19.5	52.5	87.6	150.3	308.8
External debt stocks, short-term (current US$)	27	43.5	56.1	78.4	64.3	63.9	163.9
Use of IMF credit (current US$)	5.8	13.1	10.6	12.6	22.1	15.3	30
PPG, bilateral (current US$)	53.2	88.8	182.7	225.7	202.5	180.8	197.4
PPG, bilateral concessional (current US$)	43.8	63	135.6	166.1	150.1	152.5	177.5
PPG, multilateral (current US$)	20.9	44.3	86.8	123.6	129.2	147.4	194.8
PPG, multilateral concessional (current US$)	11.9	22.5	35.5	53.4	66.6	91.4	106.7

Figure 3.2 Debt of lower-middle income countries.

Source: World Bank: World Development Indicators/Global Development Finance (WDI/GDF) Database.

countries have, and in comparing differences between Bilateral Debt and Bilateral Concessional Debt. Public and Publically guaranteed (PPG) Bilateral Debt is defined as "debt from loans from governments and their agencies (including central banks), loans from autonomous bodies and direct loans from official export credit agencies." PPG Bilateral Concessional Debt is defined as "debt from loans from governments and their agencies (including central banks), loans from autonomous bodies and direct loans from official export credit agencies. Concessional debt is defined as loans with an official grant element of 25 percent or more." (World Development Indicators/Global Development Finance series definitions). The OECD defines Official Development Assistance (ODA) as concessional if it has a grant element of at least 25 percent and is designed to promote the economic development and welfare of developing countries (OECD Development Assistance Committee (DAC) 2010). Thus some ODA lending could be categorized as PPG Bilateral Concessional Debt. Data on Multilateral debt is presented as PPG Multilateral and PPG Multilateral Concessional Debt levels (in rows eight and nine) in Figure 3.2.

Figure 3.2 depicts the changes in the composition of debt in the lower-middle income countries, and illustrates that a substantial part of the indebtedness of these countries is held by the ECAs. For example, the PPG bilateral debt indicator is the highest for the range of years listed when compared to PPG bilateral concessional, multilateral and multilateral concessional. In fact, the PPG bilateral debt is larger than the private debt levels for the years listed except for 2010 when the total debt from 2005 to 2010 almost doubles, most likely as a result of the 2008 financial crisis. Indeed, the World Bank finds that publicly guaranteed debt rose twice as fast as debt owed to private non-guaranteed borrowers in 2010, by 8 percent as compared to 4 percent (World Bank 2012: 1). While there is no distinct debt indicator representing loans from official ECAs, the previous data illustrates that a substantial part of the indebtedness of lower-middle income countries is comprised of the ECA debt.

The following sections present case studies of Ghana, Cameroon and Honduras as lower-middle income economies that made progress in reducing their debt, and reached the HIPC completion point. However, after the debt forgiveness provided at the completion point, these countries subsequently had increases in their debt burden. These case studies illustrate the processes of Paris Club rescheduling of debt, following the HIPC Initiative under which debt is forgiven, and then how these countries subsequently received export credit facilities from the ECAs of the US Export-Import Bank, the UK's Export Credits Guarantee Department and Canada's Export Development Canada.

The process of Paris Club rescheduling, reaching the HIPC completion point and subsequent ECA financing

Ghana

Ghana participated in three Paris Club reschedulings: December 10, 2001; May 16, 2002; and July 22, 2004. The US, the UK and Canada participated in all three of Ghana's Paris Club reschedulings as creditor countries. The distinction of being listed as a creditor country in the rescheduling means that these countries had claims toward the debtor country, and thus were participating in restructuring debt incurred prior to the "cutoff date." The cutoff date is established for all debtor countries when they first come to the Paris Club and is important because credits granted after this date are generally not subject to rescheduling.[9] The rescheduling process involves debt that was acquired prior to the cutoff date. Thus, participation by a creditor country in a Paris Club rescheduling agreement actually means that the creditor country has a prior history of extending ODA, non-ODA or both to the debtor country. Recent research on ODA amounts and export credit guarantees shows that there is considerable overlap between these amounts. When export credit debts are cancelled by creditor countries (in the form of debt relief), that money is transferred from aid budgets to the ECA of the creditor country in order to cover those losses (Eurodad 2011: 3, 8). Thus, debt cancellation is counted as ODA, and some of the bilateral debt that is cancelled is debt originating from export credit guarantees.

During Ghana's December 2001 rescheduling agreement, the Paris Club creditors agreed to "fix" a new cutoff date of June 20, 1999, since Ghana was expected to reach the decision point under HIPC in early 2002 (Paris Club Press Release December 10, 2001). Ghana's old cutoff date was January 1, 1983, so in effect this meant that credits granted between January 1, 1983 and June 20, 1999 could now be eligible for rescheduling. Also, the July 22, 2004 Paris Club rescheduling was Ghana's "HIPC exit treatment" and occurred after Ghana reached the completion point under the HIPC on July 13, 2004 (Paris Club Press Release July 22, 2004). Paris Club creditors agreed to cancel $821.5 million (in nominal terms) of Ghana's debt and the agreement noted that "most creditors committed on a bilateral basis" to grant additional relief to reduce the stock of debt owed to the Paris

Club creditors further by $823 million (in nominal terms). Thus, as a result of this agreement, Ghana's debt to the Paris Club creditors was reduced from $1.94 billion to $300 million (Paris Club Press Release July 22, 2004). However, even though all three of these countries participated in rescheduling Ghana's pre-cut off date debt under a Paris Club rescheduling agreement, the ECAs of these countries provided subsequent export credit facilities to Ghana, primarily beginning in 2007 (see Table 3.1).

In fact, while the US Ex-Im Bank provided a loan to the Ministry of Mines and Energy for Engineering and Procurement Services purchased from the firm Solar Outdoor Lighting Inc., on May 7, 2001, the US Ex-Im Bank did not provide any export credit facilities to Ghana again until May 31, 2007, when a guarantee was provided for a private firm to purchase oil-storage tanks and pipelines (US Ex-Im Bank Annual Reports 2001: 26; 2007: 22). However, after 2007 the Ex-Im Bank increased its scale of lending to Ghana markedly. On August 28, 2008 the US Ex-Im Bank extended a loan to a private firm for equipment for a rural electrification project and on December 12, 2008 the US Ex-Im Bank extended a loan to a private firm for water-treatment system equipment (US Ex-Im Bank Annual Reports 2008: 23; 2009: 18). Both of these loans listed the Ministry of Finance and Economic Planning of Ghana as the obligor of the loan, in other words, the Ghanan government. On February 12, 2010 and May 20, 2010 the US Ex-Im Bank extended one loan and one guarantee (respectively) for purchases by the Ministry of Finance and Economic Planning (US Ex-Im Bank 2010: 23).

Why did export credit activity to the country increase markedly after 2007? One explanation is that possibly the creditor countries believed that the country was in a less precarious debt situation beginning in 2007. According to Global Development Finance data, Ghana was granted debt relief in the amount of $4,649 million under the Multilateral Development Relief Initiative (MDRI) in 2006 so it is possible that the creditor countries believed that the country's debt situation had improved after completing the HIPC process in 2004, and then receiving additional relief under MDRI (World Bank 2012: 149). This might explain why the UK's ECGD did not provide an export credit facility to Ghana until 2008–2009 when a guarantee was provided for the domestic firm PW Ltd. to provide an airport extension to the Ghana Civil Aviation Authority (ECGD Annual Review and Resource Accounts 2008–09: 12). In addition, export credit activity from Canada's EDC only occurred after MDRI relief was provided in 2007, with a loan in order to purchase various goods and services from

Table 3.1 Ghana's Paris Club debt rescheduling and export credit activity, 2000–2012

Date	*Paris Club*	*US Export-Import Bank*	*UK ECGD*	*Canada EDC*
2000				
2001	December 10, 2001	May 7, 2001; 1 loan		
2002	May 16, 2002			
2003				
2004	July 22, 2004			
2005				
2006				
2007		May 31, 2007; 1 guarantee		
2008		August 28, 2008; 1 loan; December 12, 2008; 1 loan	2008–2009; 1 guarantee	
2009				November 26, 2009; 1 loan
2010		February 12, 2010; 1 loan; May 20, 2010; 1 guarantee		
2011				May 4, 2011; 1 guarantee
2012				May 16, 2012; 1 loan
Total number of facilities		6	1	3

Sources: Paris Club website; US Export-Import Bank Annual Reports, various years; UK ECGD Annual Reports, various years; Canada's EDC, 2011–2012 https://19.edc.ca/edcsecure/disclosure/DisclosureView.aspx?yr=2009&lang=EN; 2001–2010 data sent from EDC representative.

the domestic firm Magellan Aerospace Inc. on November 26, 2009, a guarantee to support foreign direct investment from the firm Mercator Transport International Inc. on May 4, 2011, and finally a loan to support the sale of technology in the telecommunications sector from "various Canadian exporters" on May 16, 2012 (see Table 3.1).[10]

However, from 2001 to 2012 these three ECAs provided a total of ten export credit facilities to Ghana that have contributed to the long-term debt problems of the country, especially by 2008. According to the (2012) Global Development Finance data on the debt of developing countries, Ghana's public and publicly guaranteed bilateral debt was $1,039 million in 2000, the year preceding the 2001 Paris Club rescheduling agreement. By 2005, this indicator of Ghana's debt had decreased to $316 million, and had only increased slightly in 2006 to $349 million (World Bank 2012: 149). However, by 2008, Ghana's public and publicly guaranteed bilateral debt a little more than doubled to $718 million, increased to $1,002 million in 2009 and increased to $1,360 million in 2010 (World Bank 2012: 149). The time period of 2008–2009 also coincides with higher export credit activity from the ECAs of the US, the UK and Canada. The situation regarding the increase in Ghana's debt burden is particularly problematic since Ghana completed the HIPC Initiative that was specifically designed to reduce the country's debt stocks. In fact, Ghana's total change in external debt stocks rose from –$284 million in 2005, the year after Ghana reached the completion point, to $2,038 million in 2010 (World Bank 2012: 149). While the HIPC Initiative was successful in reducing Ghana's debt there are not sufficient mechanisms in place to ensure that Ghana does not have trouble with an unsustainable debt burden in the future; especially debt resulting from export credit activity.

Cameroon and Honduras

Cameroon and Honduras were two other lower-middle income economies that also reached the HIPC completion point and had subsequent ECA activity but on a much smaller scale. In fact, the ECA activity was primarily from the US Export-Import Bank. Cameroon participated in two Paris Club reschedulings: January 24, 2001 and June 17, 2006. The US, the UK and Canada participated in both of Cameroon's Paris Club rescheduling agreements as creditor countries. Cameroon's Paris Club rescheduling on June 17, 2006 was the country's "HIPC exit treatment" and occurred after Cameroon had reached the completion point under HIPC on April 28, 2006. As a result of this rescheduling agreement (and additional bilateral assistance) Cameroon's debt to the Paris Club creditors was reduced from $3502 million to $27 million (Paris Club Press Release June 17, 2006). During the time frame 2001–2014, only the US Export-Import Bank provided an export credit facility to Cameroon. On April 11,

2012, the US Ex-Im Bank provided a guarantee for the Ministry of Economy, Planning and Regional Development to purchase road-construction machinery from the firm Hoffman International Inc. (US Export-Import Bank 2012 Annual Report: 34). Cameroon also does not have the long-term debt problems that were evident in Ghana. According to World Bank data on developing country debt, Cameroon's public and publicly guaranteed bilateral debt was $6,811 million in 2000 the year preceding the 2001 Paris Club agreement. By 2005, this indicator of Cameroon's debt had only decreased to $4,407 million, but after the country reached the completion point and had a subsequent Paris Club rescheduling in 2006, this indicator of Cameroon's debt fell substantially to $1,669 million (World Bank 2012: 101). Cameroon's public and publicly guaranteed bilateral debt had not returned to 2006 levels as of the data for 2010.

Honduras participated in two Paris Club reschedulings: April 14, 2004 and May 12, 2005. While the US and Canada participated in both of Honduras' reschedulings as creditor countries, the UK only participated as an observer. Honduras' May 12, 2005 Paris Club rescheduling was the country's "HIPC exit treatment" and occurred after the country had reached the completion point under the HIPC on April 5, 2005. Honduras had $1,473 million due to the Paris Club creditors as of March 1, 2005. As a result of the 2005 rescheduling agreement, $316 million in debt was treated, with $206 million being cancelled and $110 million was rescheduled.[11] On August 11, 2010, the US Ex-Im Bank provided a loan to a Honduran firm in the amount of $158,557,469 for the sale of wind turbines (US Ex-Im Annual Report 2010: 23). Even though the borrower in the Honduran case was a private-sector entity, because the credit was extended by an official institution, it would be discussed in the Paris Club under a rescheduling arrangement (Rieffel 1985: 2). At this point it does not appear that Honduras has substantial long-term debt problems, although debt decreases seem to have coincided with debt forgiveness under HIPC and a related program, the MDRI.

According to World Bank data on developing country debt, Honduras' public and publicly guaranteed bilateral debt was $1,423 million in 2000, and following the country's 2004 Paris Club agreement this debt indicator had fallen to $899 million in 2005. After Honduras reached the completion point in April 2005, and benefitted from a second Paris Club rescheduling, the public and publicly guaranteed bilateral debt of the country fell again to $696 million in 2006 (World Bank 2012: 163). This indicator of the country's debt also decreased slightly in 2007, to $680 million but then the debt increased again in 2008 ($833 million), 2009 ($842 million) and 2010 ($823 million) almost back to 2005 levels. In 2006 and 2007 the country also benefitted from substantial amounts of debt forgiveness during debt restructurings according to the World Bank data. In 2006, Honduras benefitted from debt forgiveness as part of restructuring in the amount of $1,511 million, and $1,193 million in 2007 under the HIPC and MDRI programs, respectively. Therefore, it is possible that the decrease in the country's public and publicly guaranteed bilateral debt could not be sustained apart from substantial debt forgiveness in the longer term although the debt level in 2010 ($823 million) had not reached the level seen in 2000 ($1,423 million) (World Bank 2012: 163).

Conclusion

Although it is not sufficiently covered in the literature on developing country debt, the debt owed to export credit agencies is certainly a major factor in the long-term debt problems of some developing countries. Research on the Paris Club debt rescheduling has documented the serial rescheduling problem and the situation whereby rescheduling does not substantially ease the debt burdens of the countries. However, not enough attention has been paid to how the public and publicly guaranteed bilateral debt levels of these countries continue to rise following the rescheduling process. Developing countries are acknowledging having difficulty paying their debt, and they turn to Paris Club creditors in order to have their stock of debt reduced, payment periods on debt extended and in some cases they are allowed grace periods before repayment begins. The creditor countries that participate in this process are clearly aware of these debt problems, but they subsequently provide new export credit loans and guarantees through their ECAs to these countries, resulting in increasing debt levels again. This results in a situation whereby developing countries are stuck in a revolving door of debt, rescheduling and more debt.

The strategies that have been developed to deal with high debt levels in developing countries are also problematic because while they ostensibly provide debt relief, in many cases the "relief" is canceling future debt payments while allowing countries to incur additional debt through export credits. Ghana's public and publicly guaranteed debt was basically decreasing from 2000–2006, and there was only one export credit facility in the form of a loan provided by the US Export-Import Bank during this time period. In fact, in 2005, and following the MDRI debt relief provided in 2006, Ghana had very low levels of public and publicly guaranteed debt. However, by 2010, this indicator of Ghana's debt had more than tripled, and there is a correlation with increased export credit activity from the three ECAs examined in this paper during 2008–2010.

Even though Ghana's debt situation is more problematic than the debt situation in Honduras, both countries were part of the HIPC Initiative and both have seen their debt levels increase following their exit from the HIPC. Chapter 4 will provide evidence to show that there is a relationship between arrangements from the IMF, the Paris Club reschedulings and the creditor country ECAs that extended those export credits.

Notes

1 A country's quota is designed to reflect a country's size in the world economy. According to the IMF (2001: 16) "the larger a country's economy in terms of output, and the larger and more variable its trade, the higher its quota tends to be." Quota reviews are also undertaken to determine changes in the strength of member states' economies. In the most recent quota review in September 2006, China's quota was increased from 2.98 percent to 3.719 percent, while the quota of the US remained around 17 percent (Weisman 2006: C4).

2 See Chwieroth (2008) for his analysis of how IMF staff operated independently in a decision to focus on the liberalization of capital accounts for their member states.

3 During an interview with an IMF economist conducted by the author, I asked whether the HIPC was fundamentally different from previous policies. The IMF economist responded that debt relief under HIPC was different because, prior to this, there was no mechanism to deal with debt from the multilateral institutions. Additionally, the economist remarked that the HIPC was developed specifically to create space for poverty alleviating initiatives (Author interview, IMF economist, June 14, 2010.)

4 Beginning in 1999, the IMF would begin to use a new lending facility, the Poverty Reduction and Growth Facility (PRGF), as a "transformation" from the Enhanced Structural Adjustment Facility (ESAF) as the primary means to provide support for low-income countries as they implement their PRSPs (Gupta et al. 2002: 1–3). As a result of the global financial crisis in July 2009, the IMF proposed to replace the PRGF with the Extended Credit Facility (ECF) to allow low-income countries greater flexibility in financing and in the preparation of the PRSP (http://imf.org/external/np/exr/facts/poor.htm).

5 These authors noted that their conclusions were similar to those undertaken by the SPA commissioned study (McGee, Levene and Hughes 2002: ix).

6 Bird and Powell (2009: 181–182) review debt relief initiatives and how ECAs were involved by noting that aid agencies of creditor countries did not want to see increases in aid budget monies for LICs used for old ECA credits.

7 All definitions are taken from the World Development Indicators/Global Development Finance series definitions.

8 The World Bank defines lower-middle income economies as having a GNI per capita of ($1,006 to $4,125) as of fiscal year 2015. (http://data.worldbank.org/about/country-and-lending-groups#Lower_middle_income) Accessed January 19, 2015.

9 In some cases it appears that the country's cutoff date can be changed by the Paris Club. On May 16, 2002, Ghana's cutoff date was changed from January 1, 1983 to June 20, 1999 due to the "small amounts of debt that would have been eligible (for rescheduling) otherwise" (Paris Club Press Release May 16, 2002).

10 CurrentinformationavailableatIndividualTransactionInformationhttps://19.edc.ca/edcsecure/disclosure/DisclosureView.aspx?yr=2009&lang=EN. Information from 2001–2010 was sent to me via e-mail.

11 http://clubdeparis.org/sections/traitements/honduras-20050512/viewLanguage/en

4 The cyclical process

The IMF, debt rescheduling and export credits

Renegotiation of adjustment programs and the repetition of adjustment loans to the same countries are common practices used by the multilateral institutions such as the IMF and World Bank. The IMF and the World Bank have long had consecutive agreements with countries for years, extending programs and allowing for additional funds to the same countries after previous arrangements have expired (Killick 1984; Easterly 2005; Vreeland 2003, 2007; Woods 2006). Reasons for this practice of providing new loans to countries even when the previous loans showed limited results in leading to economic growth or macroeconomic stability include arguments that it is done for political reasons (Thacker 1999; Woods 2003; Stone 2004; Broz and Hawes 2006), bureaucratic reasons (Vaubel 1986; Dreher and Vaubel 2004; Weaver and Leiteritz 2005) and that the process indirectly serves the vested interests of the powerful member states of the financial institutions by allowing debtor countries to continue to participate in the international economy by promoting export-led economic growth (Przeworski and Vreeland 2000; Birdsall, Claessens and Diwan 2003; Vreeland 2003; Abouharb and Cingranelli 2007).

In Chapter 3, I explained how the economic motives of the creditor country governments as seen by loans and guarantees provided by their ECAs are an important factor in the Paris Club debt rescheduling process. In this chapter I expand upon this analysis by showing how the interests of the IMF and those creditor states converge in the process of debt rescheduling and new export credits during Paris Club negotiations. The process of debt rescheduling is important to the continuation of trade credit to these countries, which serves the economic interests of the creditor states and the IMF. First, the process of the Paris Club debt rescheduling involves many of the same actors as the IMF and the World Bank processes of repeated adjustment programs and adjustment loans. Economically and politically powerful states participate in both processes, and these states have specific interests in making sure that the debtor countries remain economically solvent. The Paris Club debt rescheduling process involves the IMF more directly than the World Bank because "[a]s a precondition to Paris Club negotiations, the creditors insist that the debtor country conclude a program with the IMF" (Rieffel 1985: 8). Certainly, the powerful member states of the IMF and the World Bank have vested interests in debtor countries being able to continue participating in the international economy. However, this chapter will show how the interests of the IMF and those creditor states converge in the process of debt rescheduling and new export credits during the Paris Club negotiations.

The lending practices of the multilateral institutions

The literature on lending practices of the multilateral institutions is important to the theoretical framework of this chapter for two reasons. First, the IMF is a necessary part of this process because the Paris Club creditors require debtor countries to have a "current program with the IMF supported by an appropriate arrangement" in place before creditors will proceed with debt rescheduling (Callaghy 2010, 2002).[1] Rieffel (1985: 8) asserts, "IMF conditionality is absolutely essential to the Paris Club process, because more than any other factor, it determines the success or failure of the debt relief operation." Second, the motivations underlying the Paris Club debt rescheduling provide a new explanation for the policy making goals of the IMF. Countries would be willing to be under an IMF program so that they can benefit from debt rescheduling. In addition, showing progress in debt sustainability under an IMF program could provide for increases in the ceiling on nonconcessional borrowing (Das Papaioannou and Polan 2009: 318).

A brief history of structural adjustment and conditionality

The lending practices of the IMF changed the most dramatically in 1973 after the US ended its agreement to freely exchange gold for dollars thereby ending the fixed-exchange rate regime. In the 1970s, and most notably during the 1980s, the IMF moved to provide financing assistance to member states having balance of payment difficulties in return for agreements by borrowing countries that they would implement "structural" economic reforms as a condition for receiving the loan (Srinivasan 1988; Crockett 1992; Stewart 1995). The World Bank also began to rely heavily on structural adjustment loans with conditionality criteria during the 1980s. IMF conditionality, or more specifically, the terms of the structural adjustment policies have been critiqued on numerous grounds, primarily based on the evidence that countries following these policies saw limited economic growth and that other socio-economic indicators often declined in these countries (Przeworski and Vreeland 2000; Abouharb and Cingranelli 2006; Vreeland 2007; Blackmon 2008).

These findings pose even more interesting questions concerning the lending practices of the institutions. First, why did structural adjustment policies fail? Vreeland (2003) argues that governments participate in IMF programs so that they can blame the IMF for forcing them to implement unpopular economic reforms. He believes that the conditionality "forces" governments to change policy, allowing the governments to then treat the IMF as a scapegoat and blame the institutions for reforms that the government actually wanted to implement (Vreeland 2003: 339). Stone (2004) concludes that IMF policies failed in Africa because the program conditions were not enforced as a result of influential member states interfering to prevent consistent enforcement. Indeed, an earlier study showed that countries in Africa continued to receive tranches of loans even when the countries failed to meet the conditionality requirements (Killick 1995). Easterly (2005: 4) examines the repeated use of the IMF and World Bank adjustment loans to the same countries, as opposed to treating adjustment loans as independent events. He posits that some of the reasoning for repeated loans to the same country could be attributed to needing more than one loan for adjustment, but that some countries received upwards of 26 and 30 loans from 1980–1999. He also finds that time spent under an IMF program often exceeds 20 years, and that the probability of a subsequent loan does not decrease with the number of loans previously received (2005: 6–7). In short, Easterly concludes that even repeated adjustment lending policies were not successful. Birdsall, Claessens and Diwan (2003) find a pattern of "defensive lending" by the institutions in that new loans are often made to help borrowers service old ones.

Second, why do the institutions continue lending policies that do not have a strong record in leading to economic growth? These answers lie in the politics behind the IMF and World Bank lending.

First, there are arguments that the preferences of the most powerful states (generally the US) in the institutions explain many lending decisions. Scholars have found that policies of the IMF and the World Bank serve the political interests of the US by treating some countries more favorably in the loan process (Thacker 1999; Woods 2003; Broz and Hawes 2006; Dreher and Jensen 2007). Research has also shown that countries voting with the US in the UN General Assembly are likely to receive larger loans from the IMF (Oately and Yackee 2004; Dreher and Sturm 2006; Stone 2008). Dreher, Sturm and Vreeland (2013) find that temporary members of the UN Security Council receive fewer conditions in IMF arrangements than non-members suggesting that the influential shareholders in the IMF exchange political influence for less IMF conditionality. Copelovitch (2010a) provides evidence to show that the lending decisions of the IMF depend on the preferences of the G-5 (the US, the UK, Germany, Japan and France) when the governments of those states have strong preferences about lending decisions. This is important because he demonstrates that a group of countries (not just the US), have substantial influence over IMF lending policies and that this influence varies based on the preferences of those states.

Thus, scholars have found many explanations as to why the multilateral institutions continue loan programs for long periods of time to the same countries in spite of the fact that conditionality measures are often not followed and/or that the programs have limited success in leading to economic growth. Variations of these reasons also explain a similar process that occurs under the Paris Club debt rescheduling in which the same countries have debt rescheduled numerous times yet are still able to incur new debt from the creditor countries that agreed to reschedule their old debt. This chapter builds on the previous literature that presumes that the multilateral institutions have political/geo-strategic/economic interests in continuing lending policies and shows that creditor states under the Paris Club rescheduling also have vested economic interests in participating in this process. In addition, the powerful member states of the IMF are influencing lending decisions to the debtor countries since as creditor states they have *vested economic interests* in seeing a successful conclusion to the Paris Club agreements. I argue that the Paris Club creditors also are engaged in a form of "defensive lending" in that they want to roll over debt service due, in order to prevent default so that new export credit loans can be provided through their ECAs. Low-income debtor countries benefit from the Paris Club rescheduling so they agree to IMF loans, which are a precondition to rescheduling their debt; if they can show improvements in debt sustainability they can benefit from increases in nonconcessional borrowing.

Structural similarities between the IMF and the Paris Club

The IMF is a more formal organization than the Paris Club, although they share two important similarities. First, in the decision-making processes concerning IMF loans and debt rescheduling in the Paris Club, the voting is done on a consensus basis. Second, the G-5 countries (the US, the UK, Germany, Japan and France) exert much control over both of those processes since they are the largest shareholders in the Fund, and in the Paris Club as creditor states, they represent the largest economies having the largest share of exposure to states worldwide. In the IMF, the Executive Board (EB) exercises the most control over lending decisions. The EB is comprised of 24 Executive Directors (ED), and the largest shareholders of the Fund have the highest percentages of voting power proportional to their IMF quota contributions. Thus, the G-5 countries exercise the greatest decision making power since they each appoint their own ED and have a combined 37.37 percent of EB votes (Blackmon 2008; Copelovitch 2010a, 2010b).[2] However, IMF lending decisions only require a simple majority of EB votes (as opposed to other decisions that require majorities of up to 85 percent) and they are taken on the basis of consensus considering the voting power of the states (Woods 2003). Copelovitch (2010a: 56) argues that the largest shareholders of the Fund (the G-5) exercise control over decision-making since that group only needs the support of three other EDs for a majority in order to control lending decisions. Additionally, he extends this analysis by pointing out that the other EDs from rich countries (generally the G-7/G-10) share economic and political ties making cooperation much more likely in IMF lending decisions.

The Paris Club is not considered to be a formal organization because its membership is determined by creditor countries that choose to participate in the rescheduling procedures of debtor countries. The 19 permanent members of the Paris Club have the "largest exposure to other states worldwide" and agree to the rules and principles of the Paris Club. In practice, the countries that participate most regularly as creditor countries in the Paris Club procedures are the governments of the largest economic members of the OECD, plus Russia.[3] The 19 permanent members attend the negotiating meetings as "participating creditors" if they have claims toward the invited debtor country and as "observers" if they do not have claims.[4] At these meetings, creditors discuss among themselves a proposed debt treatment for the debtor country (while the representatives of the debtor country are out of the room) and once the debtor agrees to the terms on the components of the rescheduling package the agreement is finalized (Rieffel 1985: 18).[5] The finalized agreement also notes which countries participate as creditors and which countries participate as observers.

On the one hand, the relationship between the IMF and the Paris Club is relatively straight forward. In order to proceed with the Paris Club debt restructuring the country must have an agreement with the IMF. This has been the case since 1966 and became more formally enshrined in the Paris Club procedures in 1982 (Brown 1992: 295). Thomas Callaghy (2010: 162) explains, "[f]rom very early on, the work of the Paris Club has been tightly linked to IMF-mandated economic reform efforts, which only intensified after the Third World debt crisis broke in 1982 and structural adjustment became a more generalized term." Indeed, according to the Paris Club website in order for a country to have its debt restructured, the country must have implemented reforms "necessary to restore their economic and financial situation. This means in practice that the country must have a current program with the IMF supported by a conditional arrangement."[6] This is deemed to be necessary because the creditors want assurances that the required policy reforms will allow the country to be able to service its debts completely and on schedule, and going through the IMF is believed to be the best way to get these assurances (Rieffel 1985: 7–8).

The repetition of IMF loans and the serial rescheduling processes of the Paris Club in and of themselves are not unique and seem to coincide with longer-term debt problems of developing countries. Previous studies have shown problems with the repetition of IMF loans, including evidence showing that countries with a past history of IMF participation were more likely to return to the IMF than those without a history of IMF lending (Easterly 2005; Vreeland 2007: 56–57). Previous research on the number of Paris Club debt rescheduling agreements shows that they have increased dramatically from 1978 onwards, a fact attributed to the longer-term debt problems in sub-Saharan African countries (Klein 1987; Brown 1992: 295; Boorman 2006; Cheru 2006). Serial rescheduling has been increasing over time since, according to data provided by the Paris Club, there have been 429 agreements concluded with only 90 debtor countries during the existence of the Paris Club. However, the repetition of IMF loans and the serial rescheduling process of the Paris Club coupled with the disbursement of new export credit loans and guarantees raise questions about other motivating factors that explain this process.

Thus, the trickier part of the relationship between the IMF and the Paris Club is when the creditor states that participate in the Paris Club rescheduling process are the same powerful member states of the IMF. There are at least three reasons to believe that the creditor countries have other motivations for the debtor countries to agree to an IMF program and to participate in the Paris Club rescheduling process. First, as much of the previous research on the IMF has shown, borrowing countries often fail to meet their conditionality requirements and/or do not implement the policy reforms that the IMF requires; yet some of them continue to receive IMF loans. Second, scholars have shown that the preferences of the powerful member states in the IMF often influence funding decisions of the IMF (Willett 2006: 356; Copelovitch 2010a). Third, it is only after old loans are restructured that countries can be eligible for new credits in the form of guarantees or insurance in support of new export loans (Kuhn 1994: 24). Indeed, what is covered very little in the information about the Paris Club rescheduling process is that some countries that have their debt rescheduled (payments of principal and interest falling due) from creditor countries will then receive new export credit facilities of guarantees or loans in subsequent years from the ECAs of those same creditor countries.

Paris Club debt rescheduling

The Paris Club website explains that the following are the types of debt treated under a Paris Club agreement[7]

1 Public debt – (on the debtor side) agreements signed by the government of the debtor country; debt owed by private entities and guaranteed by public sector; (on the creditor side) credits and loans granted by Paris Club creditor governments or relevant institutions, commercial credits guaranteed by them.
2 Medium- and long-term debts (excludes short term).
3 Debts granted before the cutoff date.

The language used referencing debt that is "guaranteed" is important because it specifically refers to debt that is guaranteed or backed by an

ECA. Many credits from private lenders are guaranteed by official ECAs (this distinguishes a "guarantee" from a loan or financing) and in most cases even the debtor country is unaware as to which credits were guaranteed by an ECA until the Paris Club debt rescheduling agreement (Rieffel 1984: 91, 94; 1985: 2–3). If a debtor country defaults on a loan from a private lender that was guaranteed by an ECA, then the ECA has to pay the lender. In addition, a guarantee from an official creditor country agency means that the credit will be dealt with at the Paris Club, not the London Club, even though the credit was from a private lender.

The debt restructuring agreements include specific data about the amounts of debt treated, the terms of the agreement (Naples etc.) and the amount of pre-cutoff date Official Development Assistance (ODA) debt and pre-cutoff date commercial credits (non-ODA debt) to be rescheduled. The cutoff date is established for all debtor countries when they first come to the Paris Club and is important because credits granted after this date are generally not subject to rescheduling.[8] While the Paris Club provides comprehensive data on the debt of the debtor countries there is no information provided as to what kinds of debt and in what amounts of this debt is owed to each creditor country. The data on debt levels are not aggregated by creditor country either in totals or in a breakdown of ODA compared to non-ODA debt. Therefore, specific information on whether creditors are rescheduling ODA debt or commercial credits is not available.

However, if countries are participating as creditors in a Paris Club rescheduling agreement then they are restructuring debt incurred prior to the cutoff date. This means that the creditor country has a prior history of extending ODA, non-ODA or more likely both to the debtor country. Recent research on ODA amounts and export credit guarantees shows that there is considerable overlap between these amounts. When export credit debts are cancelled by creditor countries (in the form of debt relief), that money is transferred from aid budgets to the ECA of the creditor country in order to cover those losses (Eurodad 2011: 3, 8). Thus, debt cancellation is counted as ODA, and some of the bilateral debt that is cancelled is debt originating from export credit guarantees. Indeed, recall the policy of the UK's ECA the Export Credits Guarantee Department (ECGD) is that the Department for International Development pays ECGD on behalf of the states that have their debt forgiven through the Heavily Indebted Poor Countries Initiative (ECGD Annual Report 2004–2005: 15). The policy of Japan's ECA, the Japanese Bank for International Cooperation (JBIC) announced that starting in FY 2003, there would be a waiver on ODA loans for debt relief for countries as a result of IMF and World Bank initiatives to monitor the progress of countries toward poverty reduction. Prior to this announcement the government provided grant aid for debt relief through ODA loans.[9]

There are four countries that provide the most information about the guarantees, insurance and loans that their ECAs provide to other states: the US, the UK, Canada and Japan. The ECAs of these countries are public which means that they are governmental agencies as opposed to private insurers, such as France's ECA COFACE, Germany's ECA Euler Hermes and Italy's ECA Servizi Assicurativi del Commercio Estero (SACE). The fact that the ECAs of France, Germany and Italy are private means that they do not disclose as much information about the activities of their ECAs, although all of these ECAs operate with the financial backing of their respective governments.[10] It is also very likely that the ECAs of the US, the UK and Canada disclose information about their activities due to public pressure and/or governmental regulations.[11] In fact the US Export-Import Bank is required under Section 8 of the Export-Import Bank Act of 1945 to report information about its activities annually (US Ex-Im Bank Annual Report 2004: 16).

Empirical analysis

In order to determine the economic motives of creditor governments in IMF arrangements and the Paris Club debt rescheduling process I gathered the following information. First, I developed an original data set of countries that received debt rescheduling using data from the ECAs of the US, Canada, Japan and the UK from 2000–2012 (see Appendix A).[12] Second, I confirmed that the debtor countries received a Paris Club restructuring agreement while they were under an IMF arrangement (more on this below). Then using the data from the ECAs, I recorded the number of times that export credit guarantees or loans were provided to the debtor countries following a Paris Club agreement in which the governments of the US, Canada, Japan and the UK were participating creditors in the agreement, or whether they were observers.

For the ECAs of the US and Japan, information about participation in the Paris Club debt rescheduling was clearly indicated in the Annual Reports and was cross-checked with the data on creditor country participation in the Paris Club rescheduling on their website. In the cases of Canada and the UK, I confirmed that they were listed as creditor countries and not observer countries in the debt restructuring agreements with the various countries. Then I determined whether the countries that had debt rescheduling were subsequently provided with loans and/or guarantees from the ECAs of those countries that agreed to debt rescheduling from the sources listed below.

- The US provides information about its ECA, the US Export-Import Bank in its Annual Reports (2001–2012). In each Annual Report, there is a table listing "Paris Club Bilateral Agreements" and the countries that had debt forgiven and/or rescheduled for that year. These reports also contain "Authorizations Listings" as to which countries received guarantees, loans and insurance from US Ex-Im with amounts, and the month, day and year of approval for financial support.
- Japan provides information about its ECA the JBIC in its Annual Reports (2001–2012). However, these reports only provide information about loan commitments to countries, not guarantees, and only the year of the loan is provided.
- The UK provides information about its ECA, the ECGD in its Annual Review and Resource Accounts (2000–2012). In each report there is a "List of Guarantees Issued" as to which countries received guarantees from ECGD with amounts, but only the year in which the financial support was provided is listed.
- Canada provides information about its ECA, the EDC under "Individual Transaction Information" on the EDC website (2011–2012).[13] This data includes which countries received guarantees and/or loans from EDC with amounts, and the month, day and year of the financial support.[14]

Creditor country participation in Paris Club rescheduling and ECA activity

There were seven debtor countries (Kenya, Pakistan, Nigeria, Ghana, Indonesia, Dominican Republic and Ecuador) in which there is a recurring pattern of an IMF arrangement followed by a Paris Club debt rescheduling and subsequent loans and/or guarantees from the four creditor country ECAs during 2000–2012 (see Tables 4.1–4.7).

The next sections of the paper will provide some observations about the overall patterns seen in this process followed by more specific analysis of differences between the activities of the creditor countries.

General observations: IMF arrangements and the Paris Club

During the time period of this study (2000–2012) each of the seven countries had at least two Paris Club reschedulings (both of Pakistan's

Table 4.1 Kenya's Paris Club agreements and export credit activity, 2000–2012

Date	*IMF*	*Paris Club*	*US EX-IM loans or guarantees*	*UK ECGD*	*Canada EDC*	*Japan JBIC*
2000	ECF August 4, 2000	November 15, 2000 (all participate)				
2001						
2002			December 5, 2002; G			
2003	ECF exp. August 3, 2003 ECF November 21, 2003					1; L
2004		January 15, 2004 (active) (all participate)	May 13, 2004; F	1; G (2004–2005)		
2005			April 13, 2005; May 19, 2005; G (2)	1; G (2005–2006)	December 16, 2005; F	
2006				1; G (2006–2007)		1; L
2007			February 15, 2007; G		October 18, 2007; F	1; L
2008						
2009						
2010					November 2, 2010; G	
2011	ECF January 31, 2011		May 26, 2011; G			
2012					November 2, 2012; PRI	
Total number of facilities			**1 F; 5 G**	**3 G**	**2 F; 1 G; 1 PRI**	**3 L**

Sources: Paris Club Website; US Export-Import Bank Annual Reports, various years; UK ECGD Annual Reports, various years; Canada's EDC, 2001–2012.

Key: ECF = Extended credit facility; G = Guarantee; F = Financing; L = Loan; PRI = Political risk insurance.

Table 4.2 Pakistan's Paris Club agreements and export credit activity, 2000–2011

Date	*IMF*	*Paris Club*	*US EX-IM loans or guarantees*	*UK ECGD*	*Canada EDC*	*Japan JBIC*
2000	SBA November 29, 2000					1; L
2001	SBA exp. September 30, 2001; ECF December 6, 2001	January 23, 2001 (all participate) December 13, 2001 (active, all participate)				3; L
2002				1; G (2002–2003)		4; L
2003			February 20, 2003; G			
2004	ECF exp. December 5, 2004		August 20, 2004; G	1; G (2004–2005)		
2005			September 28, 2005; G			3; L
2006				1; G (2006–2007)		2; L
2007					October 20, 2007; G	
2008	SBA November 24, 2008		March 21, 2008; G			
2009				1; G (2009–2010)		
2010						
2011	SBA exp. September 30, 2011					
Total number of facilities			**4 G**	**4 G**	**1 G**	**13 L**

Sources: Paris Club Website; US Export-Import Bank Annual Reports, various years; UK ECGD Annual Reports, various years; Canada's EDC, 2001–2012.

Key: ECF = Extended credit facility; EFF = Extended fund facility; SBA = Stand-by arrangement; L = Loan; G = Guarantee.

Table 4.3 Nigeria's Paris Club agreements and export credit activity, 2000–2012

Date	*IMF*	*Paris Club*	*US EX-IM loans or guarantees*	*UK ECGD*	*Canada EDC*	*Japan JBIC*
2000	SBA August 4, 2000	December 13, 2000; (all participate except Canada; present as observer)				
2001	SBA exp. October 31, 2001					
2002				1; G (2002–2003)		
2003						
2004			August 6, 2004; G (FY 2005) August 9, 2004; G		November 15, 2004; G	
2005	PSI October 17, 2005 (IMF approval on October 5, 2005)	October 20, 2005; (all participate except Canada; present as observer)				
2006			February 23, 2006; April 25, 2006; G (2)			
2007	2005 PSI expires (valid from 2005–2007)				May 24, 2007; F	
2008			December 5, 2008; G (2)	3; G (2008–2009)		
2009			April 23, 2009; May 28, 2009; October 27, 2009; G (3)	1; G (2009–2010)	March 3, 2009; December 7, 2009; F (2)	
2010			February 24, 2010; G	1; G (2010–2011)		
2011				1; G (2011–2012)	January 27, 2011; E	
2012						
Total number of facilities			**10 G**	**7 G**	**1 G; 3 F; 1 E; 0 as creditor (last participation as creditor: December 16, 1986)**	**0**

Sources: Paris Club Website; US Export-Import Bank Annual Reports, various years; UK ECGD Annual Reports, various years; Canada's EDC, 2001–2012.

Key: SBA = Stand-by arrangement; PSI = Policy support instrument; G = Guarantee; E = Equity; F = Financing.

Table 4.4 Ghana's Paris Club agreements and export credit activity, 1999–2012

Date	*IMF*	*Paris Club*	*US EX-IM loans or guarantees*	*UK ECGD*	*Canada EDC*	*Japan JBIC*
1999	ECF May 3, 1999					
2000						
2001		December 10, 2001; (all participate)				
2002	ECF exp. November 30, 2002	May 16, 2002; (all participate)				
2003	ECF May 9, 2003					
2004	July 13, 2004 (HIPC completion point)	July 22, 2004; (HIPC exit active) (all participate)				
2005						
2006	ECF exp. October 31, 2006					
2007						
2008			August 28, 2008; December 12, 2008; L (2)	1; G (2008–2009)		
2009	ECF July 15, 2009				November 26, 2009; F	
2010			February 12, 2010; L May 20, 2010; G			
2011					May 4, 2011; G	
2012	ECF exp. July 23, 2012				May 16, 2012; F	
Total number of facilities			**1 G; 3 L**	**1 G**	**2 F; 1 G**	**0**

Sources: Paris Club Website; US Export-Import Bank Annual Reports, various years; UK ECGD Annual Reports, various years; Canada's EDC, 2001–2012.

Key: ECF = Extended credit facility; G = Guarantee; F = Financing; L = Loan.

Table 4.5 Indonesia's Paris Club agreements and export credit activity, 2000–2012

Date	*IMF*	*Paris Club*	*US EX-IM loans or guarantees*	*UK ECGD*	*Canada EDC*	*Japan JBIC*
2000	EFF February 4, 2000	April 13, 2000 (all participate)				5; L
2001			May 17, 2001; LNovember 15, 2001; L			11; L
2002		April 12, 2002 (all participate)	June 13, 2002; L (2)			13; L
2003	EFF exp. December 31, 2003		September 17, 2003; G (2)			10; L
2004						11; L
2005		May 10, 2005 (all participate except US; present as observer) (fully repaid)		1; G (2005–2006)		6; L
2006					December 18, 2006; F	12; L
2007				1; G (2007–2008)	January 31, 2007; G September 24, 2007; F	7; L
2008				1; G (2008–2009)	November 6, 2008; F	10; L
2009						19; L
2010						5; L
2011			March 17, 2011; G		February 18, 2011; December 22, 2011; F (2) March 31, 2011; G	15; L
2012			January 20, 2012; G March 23, 2012; G		October 3, 2012; December 5, 2012; F (2) September 25, 2012; G	
Total number of facilities			**4 L; 5 G 4 L and 5 G as creditor**	**3 G**	**7 F; 3 G**	**124 L**

Sources: Paris Club Website; US Export-Import Bank Annual Reports, various years; UK ECGD Annual Reports, various years; Canada's EDC, 2001–2012.

Key: EFF = Extended fund facility; G = Guarantee; F = Financing; L = Loan.

Table 4.6 Dominican Republic's Paris Club agreements and export credit activity, 2000–2012

Date	*IMF*	*Paris Club*	*US EX-IM loans or guarantees*	*UK ECGD*	*Canada EDC*	*Japan JBIC*
2000				1; G (2000–2001)		
2001			June 1, 2001; G (2) October 18, 2001 – July 12, 2002; G (14)	1; G (2001–2002)	December 18, 2001; G	
2002			November 26, 2002 – March 31, 2003; G (6)		January 11, 2002; F	
2003	SBA August 29, 2003			1; G (2003–2004)	December 22, 2003; F	
2004		April 15, 2004; (classic terms) (Japan/US participate; Canada UK observers)	October 7, 2004; G		November 16, 2004; December 24, 2004; F (2)	
2005	SBA exp. January 31, 2005 SBA January 31, 2005	October 21, 2005; (active) (Japan/US participate; Canada observer; UK not present)			October 20, 2005; December 22, 2005; PRI (2)	
2006					January 22, 2006; November 8, 2006; F (2)	
2007					February 28, 2007; G October 2, 2007; F	
2008	SBA exp. January 30, 2008					
2009	SBA November 9, 2009					
2010			March 4, 2010; L October 13, 2010; G			
2011				1; G (2011–2012)		
2012	SBA exp. March 8, 2012				November 1, 2012 G	
Total number of facilities			**24 G; 1 L 2 G; 1 L as creditor**	**4 G; 0 as creditor**	**2 G; 7 F; 2 PRI 0 as creditor**	0

Sources: Paris Club Website; US Export-Import Bank Annual Reports, various years; UK ECGD Annual Reports, various years; Canada's EDC, 2001–2012.

Key: SBA = Stand-by arrangement; G = Guarantee; F = Financing; L = Loan; PRI = Political risk insurance.

Table 4.7 Ecuador's Paris Club agreements and export credit activity, 2000–2012

Date	*IMF*	*Paris Club*	*US EX-IM loans or guarantees*	*UK ECGD*	*Canada EDC*	*Japan JBIC*
2000	SBA April 19, 2000	September 15, 2000 (all participate)				
2001	SBA exp. December 31, 2001					
2002					October 12, 2002; F	
2003	SBA March 21, 2003	June 13, 2003 (active) (all participate)			November 25, 2003; F	
2004	SBA exp. April 20, 2004		September 30, 2004; L		November 29, 2004; G December 15, 2004; F	
2005					August 31, 2005; F	
2006			June 22, 2006; L		October 31, 2006; December 22, 2006; G (2)	
2007					January 31, 2007; June 30, 2007; October 31, 2007; G (3)	
2008					August 31, 2008; G	
2009					February 28, 2009; G	
2010					September 30, 2010; G	
2011					January 31, 2011; March 8, 2011; G (2)	
2012					April 17, 2012; October 31, 2012; G (2) October 19, 2012; PRI November 15, 2012; F	
Total number of facilities			**2 L**	0	**5 F; 13 G; 1 PRI**	0

Sources: Paris Club Website; US Export-Import Bank Annual Reports, various years; UK ECGD Annual Reports, various years; Canada's EDC, 2001–2012.

Key: SBA = Stand-by arrangement; G = Guarantee; F = Financing; L = Loan; PRI = Political risk insurance.

occurred in 2001) and in every instance save one, they all occurred when the country was under an arrangement with the IMF. Indonesia had a third Paris Club debt rescheduling (May 10, 2005) as a result of financial problems from the 2004 Tsunami and it was the only time that a country did not have a current arrangement with the IMF; Indonesia's EFF with the IMF had expired on December 31, 2003 (see Table 4.5). This specific Paris Club agreement was significant for an additional reason. It was the only time that the US had been listed as an observer country and not as a participating creditor in the Paris Club agreement. For all other countries in this study, and for Indonesia's two previous Paris Club agreements (April 13, 2000 and April 12, 2002) the US participated as a creditor country in the Paris Club agreement, and the country had an arrangement with the IMF. Thus, it appears that in order for the US to participate as a creditor in a Paris Club rescheduling agreement, the country must have an arrangement with the IMF. This information confirms previous studies showing the importance that the US accords the IMF because of the specific macroeconomic conditionality criteria that the Fund places on countries, or for the fact that the US wants countries under an IMF arrangement so that has influence over the terms of the arrangement. In all likelihood, some combination of both reasons explain the requirement that the debtor country be under an IMF program before the US will participate as a creditor country in a Paris Club agreement.

Nigeria's experience with the IMF and Paris Club also shows the importance placed on an IMF arrangement prior to a Paris Club agreement (see Table 4.3). First, while Nigeria concluded a Stand-By Arrangement (SBA) with the IMF on August 4, 2000 prior to the Paris Club agreement on December 13, 2000, the country never drew on these funds.[15] Furthermore, on October 5, 2005, the EB of the IMF created a new policy arrangement designed to allow Nigeria to satisfy the IMF requirement needed in order to conclude a Paris Club agreement. This policy arrangement, the Policy Support Instrument (PSI) would provide "policy support and signaling to low-income countries that do not want – or do not need financial assistance from the IMF" (IMF PIN 05/145). Nigeria was then approved for a two-year PSI on October 17, 2005, and concluded a Paris Club agreement on October 20 (IMF Press Release No. 05/229; Paris Club website).

Countries are required to have an arrangement with the IMF prior to a Paris Club agreement, and the Nigerian case shows how the powerful member states of both institutions are able to work together to achieve that goal even if the debtor country does not need IMF funding. The following section extends this analysis by examining the creditor country participation in the Paris Club agreements and subsequent occurrences in which the ECAs of those creditor countries then extended new loans or guarantees following the rescheduling agreements. The data provides some evidence to indicate that the powerful member states of the IMF and the Paris Club have vested economic interests in seeing that debtor countries conclude arrangements with the IMF and debt restructuring with the Paris Club, in part, so that those countries can qualify for future export credits.

Paris Club rescheduling followed by export credit guarantees and loans

The data in Tables 4.1–4.7 show that seven debtor countries that participated in the Paris Club rescheduling received new export credit guarantees and/or loans from the ECAs of the US, the UK and Canada when they participated as creditor countries in the Paris Club rescheduling process. The US Ex-Im Bank and Canada's EDC also provide specific dates for their ECA authorizations, meaning that it is possible to see when authorizations were provided in the months following a Paris Club rescheduling during the same year. On three occasions the US Ex-Im Bank extended guarantees in the months following the Paris Club agreement, and on one occasion Canada's EDC extended a loan to Ecuador five months after a Paris Club agreement. This activity is a clear recognition of the vested economic interests involved in this process since a decision was made to provide further export credit facilities to countries in mere months following their request to reschedule their pre-cutoff date debt.

The descriptive statistics on the ECA activity indicate that the US Ex-Im Bank was the most active provider of both loans and guarantees to debtor countries, providing a total of 38 types of export credit facilities during 2000–2012, averaging 5.43 export credit facilities per country. Canada's EDC was a close second providing 37 types of export credit facilities during 2000–2012, averaging 5.28 export credit facilities per country (see Table 4.8).

Japan's JBIC is an outlier, providing 127 loans to Indonesia, 13 loans to Pakistan and three to Kenya while providing zero loans to four countries. Loans are more risky than guarantees, and the Japanese government is possibly wary of providing new loans to countries that have already requested Paris Club rescheduling of old pre-cutoff date loans.[16]

Canada and the UK did not participate as creditor countries in the Paris Club negotiations of the Dominican Republic, and Canada

Table 4.8 ECA activity during government participation as a creditor during the Paris Club agreements for selected countries (1999–2012)

ECA	*Total*	*Loans*	*Guarantees*	*Mean*	*Minimum*	*Maximum*
US EX-IM	38	10	27	5.42	2	10
Canada EDC	37	18	19	5.29	0	13
UK ECGD	18	n/a	18	2.57	0	7
Japan JBIC	140	140	n/a	20*	0	124

*Japan had 124 loans to Indonesia, 13 to Pakistan, 3 to Kenya and 0 to four countries.

did not participate as a creditor country in the Paris Club negotiations of Nigeria. According to the Paris Club website, entities listed as "observers" in the Paris Club agreements include representatives of international financial institutions or "members of the Paris Club that have no claims concerned by the debt treatment."[17] This means that either the debtor countries did not have debt from those countries (that it was requesting to be rescheduled), or that the creditor countries did not participate in the rescheduling of that debt. Canada did extend both guarantees and loans to the Dominican Republic following the Paris Club rescheduling agreements, while the UK extended one guarantee following the October 21, 2005 Paris Club agreement, and three guarantees prior to that agreement. Since creditor countries are countries that sign the agreed minutes and thus participate in the debt rescheduling, I only counted ECA activity when the country participated in the Paris Club agreement as a creditor country in the descriptive statistics provided in Table 4.8.

Paris Club rescheduling not followed by ECA facilities and IMF limits on nonconcessional finance

There were 40 countries that received the Paris Club rescheduling but did not receive subsequent export credit facilities from the creditor country ECAs of the US, the UK, Canada and Japan (see Appendix A). There are three primary explanations as to why these countries did not receive future export credit activity even though they participated in the debt rescheduling process: the ECAs were "closed" for business in the country (except for cases that "eliminate or externalize country risks"), the country was under an IMF program that included limits on nonconcessional financing and/or the country is experiencing an unacceptable level of debt distress.

ECAs are "closed" for business in a particular country for various political and economic reasons that have to do with risk involved in supporting finance. The US Ex-Im Bank publishes a Country Limitation Schedule (CLS) for all countries during various times during the year that specify the types of business that the US Ex-Im Bank is "open" in a particular country. The CLS published by the US Ex-Im Bank indicates whether support is available for up to one year (short-term); 1–7 years (medium-term); or over 7 years (long-term) and these terms of support are also noted as to whether they are for public sector risk, or for private sector risk for each country. Public sector (or sovereign) risk is the least risky because the government signs a guarantee that the state will use all of its resources to pay the loan; also referred to as a sovereign guarantee. Criteria as to whether a country is "open" in this category include the volatility of the political system, repayment history of the country, debt burden, balance of payments and its macroeconomic performance. Private sector (non-sovereign) risk is arranged with private firms and carries a higher risk, although in some cases the government of the importing country will act as a guarantor of the loan. Criteria as to whether a country is "open" in this category include the volatility of the political system, vulnerability to a foreign exchange crisis and the country's general business climate (Author interview, US Ex-Im Bank economist, October 3, 2003). Thus, the US Ex-Im Bank is "open" or willing to provide financing to a country in the short-, medium- or long-term and on a sovereign and/or non-sovereign basis determined by economic and political criteria used to assess the creditworthiness of a country (Blackmon 2011: 84–85).

The ECAs of the UK, Canada and Japan also use a similar limitation schedule including economic and political criteria to determine whether their ECAs are "open" and for what type of business in various countries, however, they do not provide time series data. Only current information is provided and updated on a regular basis. In addition, this data was not as detailed in noting whether cover was provided for the short-, medium- or long-term.[18] Therefore, I used the US Ex-Im Bank's CLS as a proxy to explain the lack of export credit activity to these countries from the other ECAs as well. In order to discern a pattern of determinants of lending, I examined the US Ex-IM Bank's CLS's from 2000–2012. For most years there were at least two CLSs for each year, with some years having as many as five.[19] For some countries, the US Ex-Im Bank demonstrated a pattern of being closed in both the public and private sector during the time frame of analysis. This was evident in countries such as the Democratic Republic of Congo (Congo DR), Guyana, Haiti, Central African Republic, Sierra Leone, Somalia and Liberia. For other countries such as Antigua and Barbuda, the US Ex-Im Bank was generally closed in the public sector, although open in the private sector. However, since the private sector carries a higher risk it is likely that firms would have to pay higher fees to secure financing in this sector. The front matter of the CLS under "General Conditions" explains, "The sector where the risk lies (public or private) and the country of the obligor or guarantor, if there is one, will generally be used for determining appropriate country limitations and fees" (US Ex-Im Bank Country Limitations Schedule January 2012: 2). For many countries the US Ex-Im Bank would only be "open" in the short-term which is the least risky because the Bank is providing financing for the export of goods as opposed to providing financing for infrastructure projects of a longer-term nature, which are more risky.

However, even when these countries were closed in the public and private sector, there was an exception for financing arrangements that "eliminate or externalize country risks" such as "asset-backed lease and financing structures involving equipment such as aircraft" (US Ex-Im Bank Country Limitation Schedule February 22, 2009: 9). This exception was listed under #13 of the "notes" section for all countries that were closed for any term of financing from the US Ex-Im Bank except for the countries that the Ex-Im Bank is legally prohibited from providing support (note #7) which are the following countries: Cuba, North Korea, Iran, Sudan and Syria. In other words, it appears that the US Ex-Im Bank makes exceptions for the aerospace sector even in countries where the Bank is not open for any other business. In fact, the guarantee that the US Ex-Im Bank provided to Pakistan on February 20, 2003 was for the sale of Boeing commercial aircraft to the Government of Pakistan even though Pakistan was listed as closed for all US Ex-Im Bank business (US Ex-Im Bank Annual Report 2003: 28). In addition, the only export credit activity that the US Ex-Im Bank provided to Ecuador on September 30, 2004 was for a loan to support the construction of a new airport by Caterpillar Inc., even though Ecuador was listed as closed for all US Ex-Im Bank business (US Ex-Im Bank Annual Report 2004: 28). Ethiopia benefitted from three guarantees from the US Ex-Im Bank for the sale of Boeing commercial aircraft on July 29, 2010, October 27, 2011 and May 31, 2012 even though the country was listed as closed in the public sector for over seven years, but not closed during the one to seven years time frame beginning on May 17, 2012 (US Ex-Im Bank Annual Reports 2010: 23; 2012: 35). In all three instances, the CLS date that was closest to the guarantee/loan date listed note #13 for Pakistan, Ecuador and Ethiopia.

The second explanation as to why some of these countries did not receive future export credit facilities is because the country was under an IMF program that included limits on nonconcessional borrowing.

This information can be found in the IMF's Monitoring of Fund Arrangements (MONA) database. For some countries under the IMF arrangements, the IMF imposes limits on nonconcessional external debt in order to "prevent the buildup of external debt to levels that might lead to debt-servicing problems in the medium term" (Das, Papaioannou and Polan 2009: 318). Exceptions can be made if the nonconcessional borrowing supports a "viable project that otherwise would not be undertaken . . . [h]owever exceptions must not affect debt sustainability, as determined by the debt sustainability framework" (ibid). In April 2005, the IMF and the World Bank developed a Debt Sustainability Assessment (DSA) for low-income countries in order to ensure that the debt of these countries remains sustainable. Countries that have limitations on nonconcessional external debt in their IMF programs are noted with a "10" in the notes section of Country Limitation Schedules (CLS) published by the Ex-Im Bank. This note "10" explains:

> When open for cover, medium- and long-term public sector transactions are subject to Ministry of Finance notification to Ex-Im Bank that the transaction is of the highest priority and would conform with IMF program limits on nonconcessional debt.
>
> (US Ex-Im Bank Country Limitation Schedule August 9, 2012: 8)

For the UK's ECGD, these limitations were noted as "subject to sustainable lending criteria."[20]

Thus, the limits on nonconcessional financing and the ranking of debt distress seem to explain most of the differences in whether ECAs provide subsequent trade finance activity especially with regard to low-income countries that were under IMF arrangements. For example, even though Kenya had a zero ceiling on its nonconcessional debt during 2003–2007, also indicated by a note "10" in the CLS, the country had a "13" in the notes section indicating financing for aerospace which was what guarantees were provided for by US Ex-Im Bank and the UK's ECGD during 2003, 2004, 2005 and 2007 (see Table 4.1). In addition, Kenya had a "low" level of debt distress and the country was regularly servicing its debt according to the DSA from August 20, 2008 through April 20, 2013 (DSA Database). Kenya was not under an IMF arrangement from 2008–2010, and when the country agreed to an ECF on January 31, 2011, the country no longer had a zero ceiling on its medium/long-term nonconcessional debt. Limits on March 31, 2011 were $450 million; June 30 2011 limits were $700 million and limits for June 30, 2013 were $2000 million (MONA Database).

Changes in these nonconcessional debt limits can also be seen in the fact that Kenya no longer had "10's" in the notes section of the CLS.

Ghana had a zero ceiling on its nonconcessional debt from 2003–2006 according to the MONA database, also indicated by a note "10" in the CLS during this time frame, and the note "10" continued until May 29, 2008.[21] From May 2008 through July 2009 there was no IMF agreement so there was no note "10." There were also two loans by the US Ex-Im Bank and one guarantee by the ECGD during this time frame. Ghana did agree to another IMF arrangement on July 15, 2009. However, by Ghana's ECF on July 15, 2009, the ceiling on its medium- and long-term debt had been raised to $300 million during 2009 and 2010, and for June and December 2011 the ceiling was increased to $800 million, before falling to $500 million by March 31, 2012 (MONA Database). During this time period Ghana had a "moderate" level of debt distress (DSA Database).

Thus these indicators on appropriate ceilings for medium- and longer-term debt limits are based on the strength of the performance of the country in servicing its debt, which would be in part measured by agreeing to reschedule the Paris Club debt. For example, according to data on low-income country debt distress classifications, countries classified as having a moderate or high risk of debt distress would have "their past record in meeting debt service obligations (as) a factor in determining the classification" (IMF and World Bank 2006: 7). A subsequent IMF publication explained that nonconcessional borrowing in countries with high debt vulnerabilities should only be made in "exceptional cases"; while space for nonconcessional borrowing for countries with lower debt vulnerabilities "can be considered more systematically" (IMF 2009: 7, 8).

For most of the countries that did not receive subsequent export credit activity after debt rescheduling, it was generally due to their being closed for business, but in all cases exceptions were made for the aerospace sector. However, if the country was "in debt distress" or at "high" risk for debt distress then there would be no room for financing. Ghana was ranked as having a "moderate" risk of debt distress and did not have a minimum concessionality grant requirement of 35 percent or higher and received subsequent financing, while others ranked as having a "moderate" risk of debt distress and also did not have a minimum concessionality grant requirement (Georgia, Guyana, Nicaragua and Togo) did not receive subsequent financing. Countries ranked as having a "low" level of debt distress with no minimum grant element (Congo, Honduras, Madagascar, Moldova, Senegal and Zambia) did not receive subsequent financing.

Ethiopia's level of debt distress improved over time and may have been a factor in the country's resumption of export credit activity at least through US Ex-Im Bank. In July 2008, Ethiopia's DSA level of debt distress was ranked as "moderate" (Joint IMF/World Bank DSA Ethiopia July 1, 2008). However, by May 2010 the country's DSA debt distress was ranked as "low", and the country did benefit from subsequent financing in the form of guarantees from US Ex-Im Bank in 2010, 2011 and 2012 for the sale of Boeing commercial aircraft (Joint IMF/World Bank DSA Ethiopia May 26, 2010; US Ex-Im Bank Annual Reports 2010: 23; 2012: 35). Although, as noted previously, the aerospace sector is listed as an exception for financing and Ethiopia only benefitted from financing from US Ex-Im Bank, not the other ECAs. However, the Ethiopian case provides additional support for the case that the level of debt distress does impact subsequent trade finance activity, and that if a country manages its debt, export credit activity can be resumed. To be sure, the varied circumstances of these countries mean that many of the decisions that the IMF would make about program limits and debt distress levels are made based on subjective criteria.

Conclusion

This chapter has added to the explanations as to why the IMF continues its process of repeated loan programs to the same countries by showing that there is a relationship between the IMF loans, the Paris Club debt rescheduling and the extension of new export credit facilities to those debtor countries. In addition, there is some evidence that low-income debtor countries (Kenya, Ghana) that can show progress in managing their debt levels while under an IMF program can have their limits on nonconcessional lending increased, thereby allowing for increased ECA activity as well as other commercial lending. The empirical analysis shows that some of the debtor countries that participated in the Paris Club rescheduling received new export credit guarantees and/or loans from the ECAs of the US, the UK, Canada and Japan when those countries participated as creditor countries in the Paris Club rescheduling process. While these ECAs have been the most heavily profiled in this and in previous chapters, this is primarily because these ECAs provide the most information on their financing activities. It is highly doubtful that other private ECAs do not behave in the same manner; information about their finance and lending activities is simply limited. Chapter 5 will document the role played by ECAs in providing trade finance and medium- and longer-term export credit insurance in order to increase trade during the 2008 financial crisis.

Appendix A

Debtor countries that received the Paris Club debt rescheduling (not forgiveness) but not subsequent export credit facilities 2000–2012 (total of 37 countries); According to Annual Reports of Creditor Country ECAs of the US, the UK and Japan (Canada's information is from the Paris Club information on creditor countries and cross checked with information from the Department of Finance website on countries provided with debt relief)

Antigua and Barbuda	Macedonia
Bosnia and Herzegovina	Madagascar
Burundi	Malawi
Central African Republic	Moldova
Congo	Montenegro
Cote d'Ivoire	Nicaragua
Democratic Republic of Congo	Niger
DRC Zaire	Rwanda
Gabon	Senegal
Georgia	Serbia
Grenada	Serbia and Montenegro
Guinea	Seychelles
Guyana	Sierra Leone
Haiti	Sri Lanka
Iraq	Togo
Jordan	Ukraine
Kyrgyz Republic	Yugoslavia
Liberia	Zambia
Libya	

Notes

1 http://clubdeparis.org/sections/composition/principes/cinq-grands-principes
2 http://imf.org/external/np/sec/memdir/eds.aspx
3 The following are countries listed as permanent Paris Club members: Australia, Austria, Belgium, Canada, Denmark, Finland, France, Germany, Ireland, Italy, Japan, the Netherlands, Norway, Russian Federation, Spain, Sweden, Switzerland, the UK, the US. http://clubdeparis.org/sections/composition/membres-permanents-et/membres-permanents
4 http://clubdeparis.org/sections/composition/fonctionnement-du-club/reunions
5 http://clubdeparis.org/sections/composition/fonctionnement-du-club/deroulement-d-session

6 http://clubdeparis.org/sections/services/faq/77-forum-aux-questions
7 http://clubdeparis.org/sections/dette-traitee-en-club/categories-de-dette/definition-dette
8 Recall that in the previous chapter, the Paris Club changed Ghana's cut off date from January 1, 1983 to June 20, 1999 due to the "small amounts of debt that would have been eligible (for rescheduling) otherwise" (Paris Club Press Release May 16, 2002).
9 http://jica.go.jp/english/news/jbic_archive/autocontents/english/news/2002/000061/
10 Even though the ECAs of Germany, France and Italy are private companies their medium- and long-term export credit business, which is the only type of export credit activity rescheduled by the Paris Club (the Paris Club does not reschedule short-term export credit insurance) is underwritten on behalf of their governments (Stephens 1999: 88).
11 I received information from the UKs ECGD for the years 2000–2004 via a Freedom of Information Request (e-mail correspondence).
12 The US provides information about the transaction activity of the US Ex-Im Bank in the Annual Reports of the US Ex-Im Bank. However, the US Ex-Im Bank did not include information about the Paris Club rescheduling until 2001. Canada's disclosure policy took effect in 2001 so only transactions from that date onward are provided. I received information about the list of transactions from Canada's EDC for the years 2001–2010 via e-mail correspondence since this data was no longer on the EDC website. I did not receive confirmation of rescheduled amounts from the government of Canada, so I used data from the Paris Club on Canada's creditor country participation but this may also include debtor countries that had their debt forgiven. Japan's JBIC has their Annual Reports posted on their website from 2000 onward. The UK's ECGD provides information about guarantees in their Annual Review and Resource Accounts publications and I requested and received some additional information from the UKs ECGD for the years 2000–2004 via a Freedom of Information Request.
13 Information from 2001–2010 was sent to me via e-mail.
14 CurrentinformationavailableatIndividualTransactionInformationhttps://19.edc.ca/edcsecure/disclosure/DisclosureView.aspx?yr=2009&lang=EN. Information from 2001–2010 was sent to me via e-mail.
15 See Vreeland (2007: 60–61) for additional analysis of Nigeria's experience with the IMF.
16 There could also be geo-strategic considerations for Japan's higher level of involvement with Indonesia and Pakistan.
17 http://clubdeparis.org/sections/services/glossaire/definitions/?letter=o
18 https://gov.uk/country-cover-policy-and-indicators
19 Data available at http://exim.gov/tools/countrylimitationschedule/cls-historical-reference.cfm
20 https://gov.uk/country-cover-policy-and-indicators
21 Ghana was granted a waiver for the loan made by US Ex-Im on May 7, 2001 which was for "engineering and procurement services" from the firm Solar Outdoor Lighting Inc. (MONA Database; US Ex-Im Annual Report 2001: 26).

5 Increasing trade during the crisis

The 2008 Global Financial Crisis affected financial institutions and markets worldwide resulting in a 12 percent decline in trade volumes, the largest since World War II (International Chamber of Commerce (ICC) 2010). Economists have provided various reasons for trade declines, and most of these explanations involve problems with trade finance and export credit insurers. Researchers examined the severe decline in trade and concluded that there was a link between the effects of the banking crisis on export growth (Amiti and Weinstein 2009; Iacovone and Zavacka 2009). Specifically, these studies and others (Auboin 2009; Asmundson, Dorsey, Khachatryan, Niculcea and Saito 2011) found that the scarce availability of trade credit could be responsible for the decrease in the volume of exports.

Surprisingly, political scientists have not examined the role of export credit insurers during this crisis. In this chapter, I will illustrate how the OECD ECAs supplemented trade financing and provided medium- and longer-term export credit insurance in order to increase trade during the 2008 financial crisis. In previous crises governments used ECAs in order to facilitate trade in specific circumstances (Wang and Ronci 2005). For example, during the 1997 Asian financial crisis, many ECAs provided support for trade related transactions with affected countries. The Japanese Bank for International Cooperation (JBIC) used financing to support letters of credit for the export of Japanese goods into Indonesia (Staff Team from JBIC 2005). The US Ex-Im Bank also provided short- and medium-term credit support for the export of goods and services to Korea, Thailand and Indonesia during this crisis (Starr 2005: 72–74). Sections of Chapter 2 also explained that in the early and mid-1990s the ECAs were used to facilitate trade to the former Soviet Union republics since private sector finance was either unavailable or was too expensive. However, the 2008 crisis was unique because instead of a lack of trade finance in one state or region, the problem was more systemic and was affecting all flows of international trade.

The importance of trade

There are three explanations as to why states, and especially the OECD member states, would turn to the financing mechanisms of the ECAs during the 2008 crisis. First, private sector finance was not available for simple and common trade transactions such as letters of credit. Letters of credit guarantee payment between an importer and exporter through each of their banks. Problems in trade finance began to occur in the spring of 2008 when letters of credit were not being routinely endorsed by commercial banks (Auboin 2009: 8). Primarily, this was because in the context of the sub-prime mortgage crisis, trade credits were no longer seen as different from other loans by creditors and would be subject to the same risk conditions (WTO 2008). For example, the bank issuing the letter of credit assumes the risk of default by the importer as long as the terms and conditions of the letter of credit are met (Stephens 1999: 93). Problems arose when private sector banks were no longer willing to accept these risks at the rising costs, resulting in problems in financing international trade. According to a survey of advanced, emerging market and developing country banks about trade financing conditions in 2008 conducted with the IMF and the Bankers' Association for Finance and Trade (BAFT) more than 70 percent of respondents reported that the prices of various types of letters of credit rose since late 2007; increasing the cost of trade finance (Dorsey 2009: 18–19). As a result, discussions began about government-backed institutions, namely the ECAs being used to fill the gaps in trade finance (Auboin 2009: 9). Indeed, the OECD surveys of the ECAs in selected OECD countries reported that new commitments by these ECAs had increased by 30 to 50 percent (OECD 2009).

International trade is crucial to the viability of export industries and to the economic viability of most states today. The fact that trade levels were declining due to financing problems was an unacceptable situation to governmental leaders since national economies have become increasingly integrated through trade (Mittleman 2000). Indeed, many governments have become much more involved in the economies of their states during this crisis, even in some areas that heretofore had not seen government involvement (Reich 2009; Setser

2009: 36). For example, the UK government has majority ownerships in many formerly private sector banks including the Royal Bank of Scotland (RBS). In the latter part of 2008, the US government also bought preferred equity stakes in some of the country's largest banks including Goldman Sachs, J.P. Morgan Chase, Citigroup and Bank of America (Solomon et al. 2008).[1] The US also nationalized Fannie Mae, Freddie Mac and was in the process of taking steps to unwind Washington Mutual as of mid-2008. The main reason for greater governmental involvement in the financial sector was to supplement the lack of capital available to the banks and also to provide financial stimulus in order to restore confidence in the financial sector. Thus, it is not too surprising that states would also take steps to become more involved in providing finance directly through their ECAs in order to facilitate domestic exports. Indeed, as pointed out by Auboin (2009: 19) "[t]he largest members of the international community have been able to mobilize their export credit agencies – the US, EU, Japan, Canada, Korea, China – to help compensate for shortages of trade finance from traditional, commercial bank sources."

Second, guidelines and requirements for public or governmental ECAs are very different than those for commercial banks and private ECAs. For example, in most cases governmental or public ECAs are only expected to break even, and most of them in the past have operated with recurring cash flow deficits (Kuhn, Horvath and Jarvis 1995: 8–9). From a political standpoint this is possible because ECAs are relatively unknown by the majority of a country's taxpaying citizens, thus it is easy for governmental leaders to use their resources and not expect much of a backlash.[2] It is also relatively easy for these leaders to change the financing mechanisms of their ECAs and to reallocate money to them without much attention. In fact, this chapter will illustrate that the G-7 states would make changes to the financing structures of their ECAs, and to establish foreign currency reserve lines through their central banks specifically to provide trade financing.

The third explanation as to why states would turn to ECAs during the crisis is because the use of these agencies allows states to address their particular export and financing needs without resorting to "unfair" trade distorting measures (Baldwin and Thompson 1984). One of the debates in the literature on economic globalization concerns whether states are losing their sovereignty in this newly interconnected world or whether they still retain some degree of autonomy in decision-making about trade policy. While some find that the state's power is reduced (Clark 1999; Weiss 1999; Giddens 2000), others conclude that the state and the influence of domestic politics are still important in examining the processes of economic globalization through trade (Rosenau 1997; Bhagwati 2004; Glatzer and Rueschemeyer 2005; Altman 2009). This is important because it implies that states are not held captive to the forces of economic globalization; and that in fact they will change their domestic policies in order to alleviate the negative effects of open markets (Ruggie 1982).

However, there are both formal and informal limitations on the power of states to enact domestic policy concerning trade as seen through the membership of states in Intergovernmental Organizations (IGOs) specifically concerned with trade policy.[3] This chapter will contribute to this growing literature on the relationships between the IGOs and states in trade policy because the OECD ECAs have numerous limitations and formal and informal rules that they must follow with regard to medium- and long-term export credit arrangements (Hodgson 2005; Wang and Tadesse 2005: 9). Indeed, the OECD states enacted numerous measures in order to deal with the credit crisis but these measures stayed within the boundaries of the OECD's "Arrangement on Guidelines for Officially Supported Export Credits" first established in 1978 and described in Chapter 1.

The OECD Arrangement

The OECD Arrangement acts as an international "regime" since it is a set of "principles, norms, rules, and decision-making procedures around which actor expectations converge in a given issue-area" (Krasner 1983: 1; Moravcik 1989). Under the Arrangement, the OECD member states "provide a framework for the orderly use of official export credits" thereby "reducing subsidies and trade distortions related to officially supported export credits" and disclose this information to the OECD Secretariat.[4] Recall that these limits were necessary in order to prevent an export credit subsidy war between the largest developed countries; a race to the bottom based on which country could offer the cheapest interest rates of credit for the export of their goods (Moravcsik 1989: 180–181; Stephens 1999).

While the Arrangement is not a formal body of law, it acts as a general agreement whereby member states agree to set limits and disclose information about officially-backed export credits extended for a time period of over two years. Indeed, Levit (2004: 67–68) shows that the cooperation under the Arrangement has produced a high level of compliance among its members. Thus, it is by providing and sharing this information through meetings held under the auspices of the OECD, that the members are able to alleviate concerns about unfair competition.

The OECD Participants to the Arrangement also disclosed information about what actions they were taking regarding ECA activity during the crisis (OECD 2009). Indeed, the 2008 financial crisis has been described as an event that "has put the advantages of officially-backed export credits in the spotlight" (OECD 2011: 147). The OECD agreed to host regular meetings to exchange information and monitor progress to coordinate export credit support in order to increase international trade during the crisis.[5] For example, in January 2009, the financial crisis was first addressed in a "special meeting" during which they agreed to adjust some of the principles of the Arrangement relating to project-financing types of transactions. These transactions involve medium- and longer-term financing arrangements which fall under the purview of the Arrangement. However, at this meeting it was also determined

> [i]n order to *maintain transparency and to foster a fruitful exchange of views* on the most appropriate responses brought to the financial crisis in the context of export credits, the Participants to the Arrangement also decided to *explain the measures they have taken at the national level*; these measures are reflected in a synthesis document as at 30 June 2009 [emphasis added].[6]

This document titled "Officially Supported Export Credits and the Financial Crisis: Measures Taken at the National Level by the Participants to the Arrangement, as at 30 June 2009" clearly defines and explains all of the measures taken by the Participant states regarding the provision of export credit insurance during the financial crisis.[7] The following sections of the chapter will examine trade and lending trends leading up to the 2008 crisis and will show how financing by ECAs increased, in this case, to alleviate the gap in private sector finance. This data will illustrate that the OECD states, and the G-7 states in particular, became much more involved in providing financing directly through their ECAs to lessen the severity of the declines in trade surrounding the financial crisis.

Trade finance and the 2008 financial crisis

Trade and medium- and long-term export credit volumes

In examining data on trade levels from 2000–2010, we can see that overall trade (defined as the world export of goods) has increased every year from 2003–2008 (see Figure 5.1).

The OECD states also comprise the largest share of trade as compared to the developing or emerging markets commonly referred to as Brazil, Russia, India and China (BRICs) for the years 2000–2010; although there is a trend in the BRICs gaining in their share of world exports. The percent of total OECD merchandise trade was 75.6 percent for 2006, 74.4 percent for 2007 and 74.1 percent for 2008. However, among the OECD states, the G-7 states comprised the largest percentages of trade for those years. The G-7 composition of merchandise trade was 45.5 percent for 2006, 43.9 percent for 2007 and 43 percent for 2008 (OECD 2010b).[8] In order to determine whether there is a correlation between decreases in exports from the G-7 and an increase in export credit volumes provided by the G-7, it is necessary to compare the trends in exports from the G-7 countries and G-7 export credit volumes (see Figures 5.2 and 5.3).

Comprehensive data for new medium- and long-term (two years or more) official export credit volumes extended by the G-7 countries

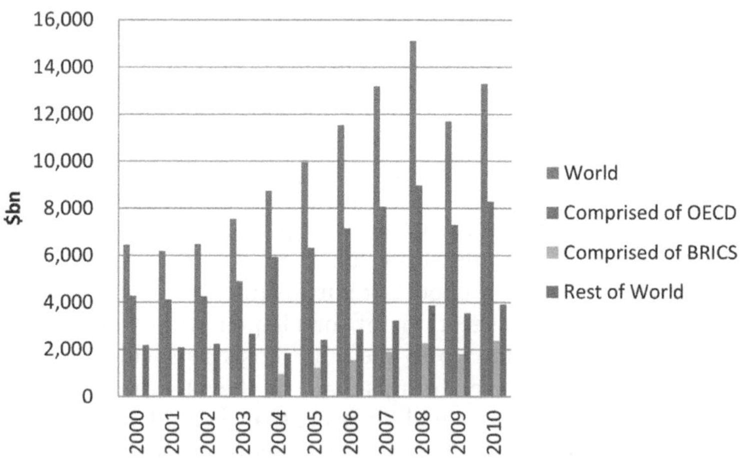

Figure 5.1 World exports of goods, 2000–2010 ($bn).

Sources: US Export-Import Bank Credit Competition Reports 2006: 7; 2009: 9; 2010: 10.

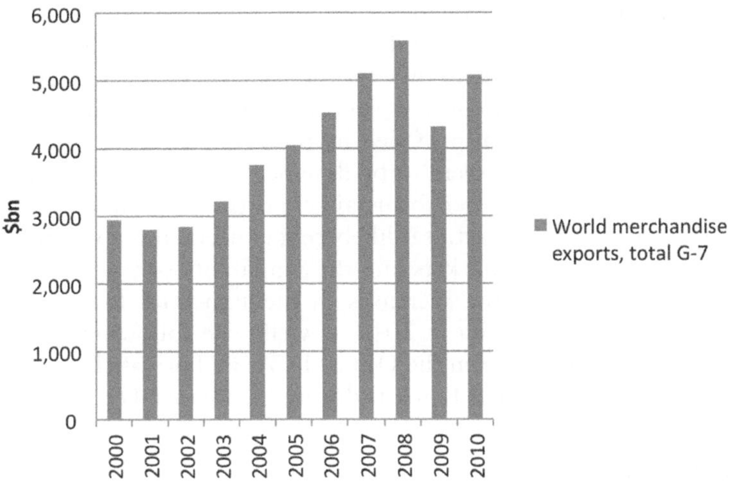

Figure 5.2 Total G-7 world merchandise exports, 2000–2010 ($bn).

Sources: World Trade Organization, International Trade Statistics, 2006; 2010 Table A6 (data on individual countries compiled by the author).

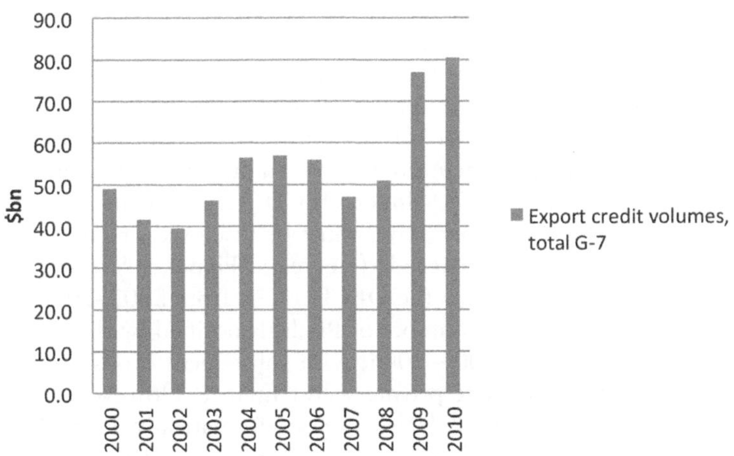

Figure 5.3 New medium- and long-term export credit volumes, total G-7, 2000–2010 ($bn).

Sources: US Export-Import Bank Export Credit Competition Reports, 2005: 8; 2010: 11.

from 2000–2008 indicate that these export credit volumes decrease or stay about the same when world exports increase. Conversely, when exports decreased from 2008–2009 official medium- and long-term export credit volumes show a growth rate of 43 percent (see Figures 5.2 and 5.3).[9] Thus, the data in Figures 5.2 and 5.3 show a correlation between a decrease in exports from the G-7 (2008–2009) and a subsequent increase in new official export credit volumes for the medium and long term provided by the G-7 during 2008–2009. Increases in export credit seem to be designed to alleviate the gap in private sector finance in order to sustain exports of a credit period of longer than two years. In fact, it is likely that concern about the future stability of the financial markets and the availability of trade finance specifically, resulted in the increases in medium- and longer-term official export volumes seen in 2010 as well. The following section examines differences between the OECD ECAs and private lenders in providing Project Finance (PF) loans during the financial crisis.

Project Finance (PF) loans

PF loans are secured by the ECAs but are different than other types of financing arrangements because financing is determined by the viability and thus the cash flow of the project itself as security for repayment. The creditworthiness of the borrower is not the only factor considered in the lending decision, and in fact, the lender in most cases is prohibited from accessing assets of the project sponsor to repay the debt; the only area of recourse would be the earnings from the project itself (Stephens 1999: 94, 104; US Ex-Im Bank Competitiveness Report 2010: 37). PF arrangements are for large infrastructure or major capital related projects; thus, their financing structure is of a long-term nature (Kuhn et al. 1995: 37). Under OECD Arrangement rules, PF deals from the OECD member states must be disclosed or "notified" only if the repayment term exceeds five years. Figure 5.4 shows the number of PF deals notified by the OECD ECAs from 2002–2010.

Figure 5.4 shows that the number of PF deals notified by the OECD ECAs is unchanged from 2004–2005; with subsequent drops in 2006 and 2007 indicating adequate private sector finance. However, beginning in 2008 the number of PF deals increases dramatically. From 2007 to 2008 the number of PF deals jumps from five to 15, and the number of deals continues to increase to 21 deals in 2009 and to 25 deals in 2010. The huge spike from 2007 to 2008 is the result of the lack of liquidity during the financial crisis, and thus the need for the ECA financing for large infrastructure projects. In all likelihood, the total number of PF loans during this time period is actually higher since these numbers represent only the loans requiring repayment terms longer than five years.

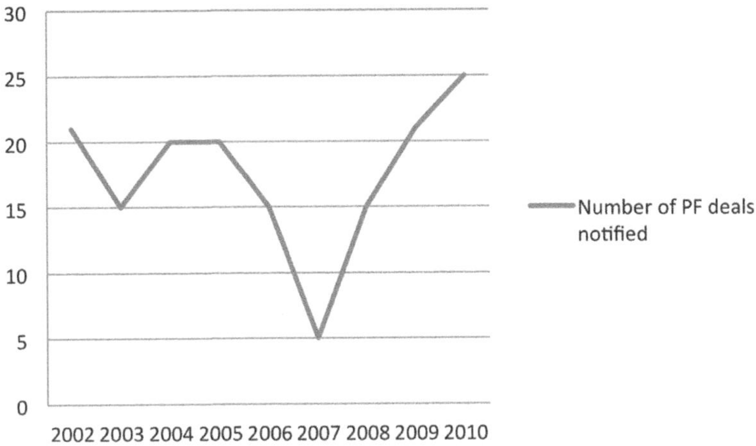

Figure 5.4 Number of PF loans from OECD ECAs, 2002–2010.

Sources: US Export-Import Bank Export Credit Competition Reports, 2006: 33–34; 2010: 37.

Another way to assess whether the OECD ECAs were providing PF loans due to the lack of private sector finance during the crisis is to examine whether the amounts of the PF loans provided by the OECD ECAs changed during the crisis. Beginning in 2006, the US Ex-Im Competitiveness Reports break down the amounts of PF Loans by "originator" meaning whether they were financed by the OECD ECAs or through private lenders.

This information confirms the trend of increases in the PF loan amounts from private lenders until 2009, with the inverse trend of small amounts of the PF loans from the OECD ECAs also until 2009. Indeed, the OECD ECA PF loans increased from $3.4 billion in 2008 to $11.1 billion in 2009 (see Figure 5.5). Thus, the shift in financing of the PF loans from private lenders to OECD ECA finance seen in 2009 (rather than 2008) is indicative of concerns about the availability of trade finance in the future. In other words, the data represent more of a lagged effect from the 2008 crisis. As noted in the US Ex-Im 2005 Competitiveness Report, "The project finance industry is cyclical in nature and is affected by the strength of the world economy and of key industries" (2005: 35). These figures provide evidence indicating that there was a need to increase PF loans during the crisis and that the OECD ECAs used these loans as an additional way to provide trade financing due to decreases in liquidity from private lenders for

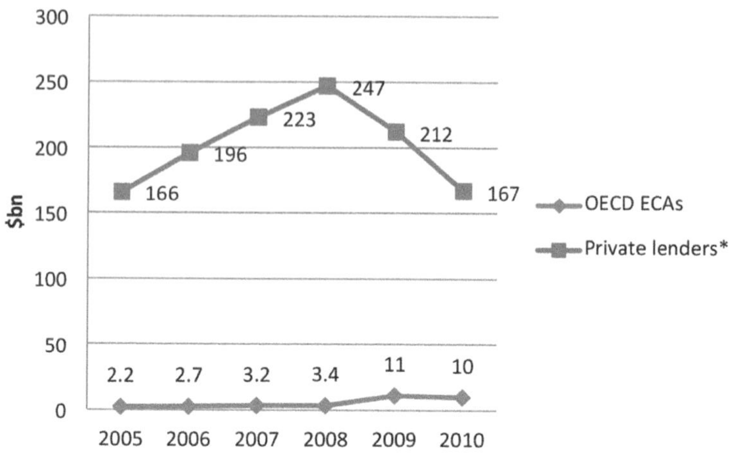

Figure 5.5 Amount of PF loans by originator, 2005–2010 ($bn).

Sources: US Export-Import Bank Export Credit Competition Reports, 2005: 34; 2010: 37.

Note: *For 2005, 2006 this category was labelled as "Non-ECA."

longer-term financing deals. The following sections examine specific changes in financial flows and export credits extended to developing countries during the 2008 crisis.

Net capital flows into emerging markets

As discussed in previous chapters, export credits are primarily designed to facilitate the export of domestic goods to developing markets and emerging economies. This has also been the case in previous time periods with regard to trends in export credit activity. For example, the 2005 US Ex-Im Bank Competitiveness Report noted that private capital flows to emerging markets rose considerably from 2004–2005 and that "a significant factor impacting (the small increase of) ECA activity levels during 2005 was the high degree of private sector involvement with respect to emerging markets" (US Ex-Im Bank Competitiveness Report 2005: 8). For that same time period (2004–2005), comparable new medium- and long-term official export credit volumes extended by the G-7 only increased modestly from $56.4 to $57 billion (see Figure 5.2). Factors attributed to the increase in private flows to emerging markets included structural reforms, greater overall stability and "higher than normal liquidity" (ibid., 9).

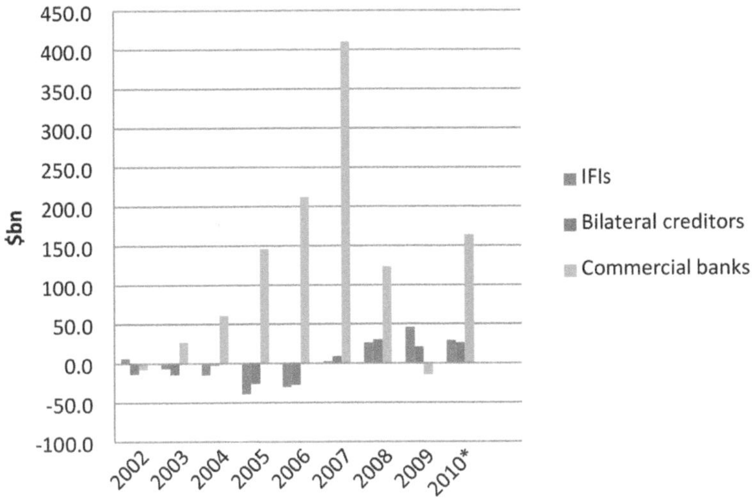

Figure 5.6 Net external capital flows into emerging markets, 2002–2010 ($bn).

Sources: US Export-Import Bank Export Credit Competition Reports, 2005: 8; 2010: 12.

Note: *Estimates.

Indeed, Figure 5.6 shows that from 2004 to 2005 flows from commercial banks increased dramatically from $61 billion to $146 billion, and continued to increase until 2008.

This figure also illustrates a trend which shows that as flows from commercial banks increase, flows from International Financial Institutions (IFIs) and bilateral creditors (which include the ECAs) decrease. Conversely, when flows from commercial banks decreased markedly in 2008, flows from the IFIs and bilateral creditors increased. Astonishingly, while flows from commercial banks into emerging markets were $410 billion in 2007, they dropped to only $123 billion in 2008, a decrease of 70 percent. In 2009, commercial bank flows to emerging markets registered no new lending.

One explanation as to why export credits would increase to developing countries in this crisis is that, "[t]rade finance is costlier and somewhat harder to get in emerging markets – where much of the intraregional trade is in low-profit-margin items that are part of the manufacturing supply chain for exports to advanced economies" (Dorsey 2009: 18). During this crisis, banks (in advanced and emerging economies) also tightened their lending guidelines (increasing the price of trade finance) due to fear of default of the

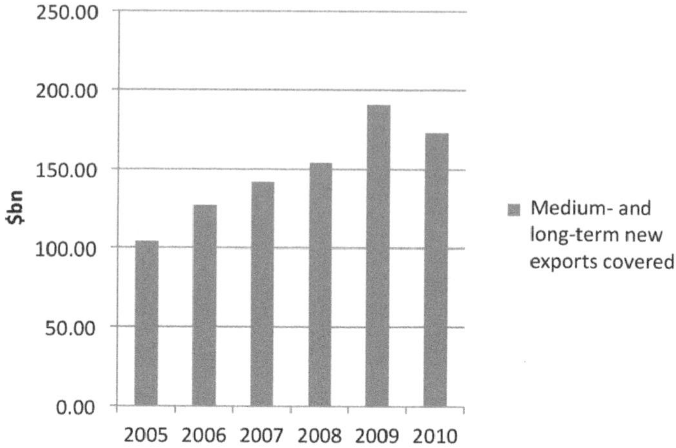

Figure 5.7 Medium- and long-term new exports covered, 2005–2010 ($bn).
Sources: Berne Union Statistics data.

specific counterparty bank. This is a type of commercial risk the ECAs provide insurance against, called counterparty risk (Dorsey 2009).

Finally, according to Berne Union data about medium- and longer-term export credit cover during this crisis, public ECAs that are members of the Berne Union provided significant medium- and longer-term cover during this crisis as compared to previous years (see Figure 5.7)

The support provided by public ECAs during this crisis was noted as crucial since these particular ECAs "carried the full faith and credit of their respective governments; a security that was sought after, especially during this crisis" (Morel 2010: 16). In fact, the amount for medium- and longer-term covered exports at $191 billion during 2009, was the highest ever recorded (Morel 2010: 16). By many measures it seems clear that the trade finance and export credit insurance provided by the ECAs helped alleviate the problems of liquidity seen during the crisis and helped to sustain international trade.

Conclusion

The 2008 crisis threatened trade finance and international trade flows. OECD member countries, and especially the G-7 countries – the countries highly dependent on trade – responded to the severe drop in international trade volumes by providing financing through their

ECAs. This chapter has demonstrated that states still have an important role to play in supporting their national economies by directing resources through their ECAs. Also, by directing resources through their ECAs states were playing by the rules of trade finance dictated by the OECD. This option is more desirable than currency manipulation to encourage exports or the implementation of trade protection policies.

Notes

1 Other governments that took control of a substantial share of banking activity included Iceland, Ireland and the Netherlands (OECD Economic Outlook 2009, Issue 1: Table 1.5).
2 In January 2012, President Obama announced that he wanted to fold five separate trade and business agencies, one of these being the US Export-Import Bank, into one single agency that would replace the Commerce Department. There was little to no public reaction to this announcement (Landler and Lowrey 2012).
3 For current research on the importance of international organizations and the role that states play in them more generally, see Abbott and Snidal 2010; Stone 2011.
4 http://oecd.org/tad/xcred/participants.htm
5 http://oecd.org/tad/xcred/exportcreditsandthefinancialcrisis.htm
6 http://oecd.org/tad/xcred/exportcreditsandthefinancialcrisis.htm
7 In e-mail correspondence with Mr. Jean Le Cocguic, of the Export Credits Division at the OECD, I asked whether any additional information about the measures taken by Participant states was available and he informed me that any public information on measures taken by Participant states was on the export credits website (personal e-mail correspondence with the author, July 1, 2014).
8 The data for this table are from 2001–2010 (OECD Factbook 2010).
9 Comprehensive data on export credits is extremely difficult to find. Kuhn et al. 1995 is a comprehensive analysis of export credits and they use Berne Union data as well as OECD data. They also devote Appendix II (39–41) of their publication to "problems that arise in analyzing the volume of export credits from the available statistics" (4). Problems with OECD statistics include the fact that the organization relies on the individual agencies for data and that each agency uses concepts and definitions for reporting data that are not consistent across agencies. Data from individual agencies is problematic because agencies are more likely to report data that is most similar to the way in which they keep their own accounting methods (Kuhn et al. 1995: 39). For example, the data used for Figure 5.3 are taken from the US Ex-Im Bank Competitiveness Reports 2005, 2010. However, these publications include data on export credit volumes that are unavailable to the general public, and unavailable to non-OECD member states. As a result of the author's personal conversation with an Ex-Im Bank economist, this person confirmed that the data include public and private export credits with terms of two years or more to all countries (developed and

developing), for all sectors and all activity including project finance loans. This person also confirmed that some of the data is from confidential sources and stated that all of the aforementioned information was why references provided for this data were non-existent or limited (Author's personal conversation with US Ex-Im Bank economist, January 13, 2012). This explanation is provided because the volume of export credit activity in publicly available OECD data used in subsequent sections of the chapter is lower than these volume amounts because the OECD data are only comprised of export credits extended to developing countries, not developed countries.

Conclusion

This book has shown that government-supported ECAs have facilitated international trade under many circumstances. In addition, there are clear connections between developing country debt incurred as a result of export credit activity, the Paris Club rescheduling of that debt, and the role of the IMF arrangements and creditor country government involvement in all of these areas. Indeed, it should be evident that scholars of international political economy need to be paying more attention to trade finance and the role of the ECAs in supporting that type of finance. In this concluding chapter I will provide four reasons as to why government-supported ECAs will become even more important in facilitating international trade over time.

Trends in international trade and finance

First, the trends of globalization and the increasing interconnectedness of states will only serve to enhance the necessity and ease of international trade. According to the WTO statistics, the volume of world exports has more than quadrupled from 1980 to 2011, with most of the growth attributed to increases in shipments of manufactured goods (WTO 2013: 67). In fact, while exports of manufactured goods have seen a six-fold increase since 1980, exports of agricultural goods only increased 2.6 times (WTO 2013: 67). This trend of consistent increases in international trade in manufacturing evident since the 1980s, will also result in a greater reliance on government-supported ECAs in order to sustain trade increases, especially to developing countries. According to the WTO, the share of North–South trade in world merchandise exports was only 33 percent in 1990, but had increased to 38 percent by 2011. Conversely, North–North trade has declined over this time frame from 56 percent in 1990 to 36 percent in 2011(WTO 2013: 65)

I argue that increases in international trade, especially manufactured goods, will continue and that the trend of North–South trade will increase, and that these trends will be assisted by governmental ECAs. Recall that while the first ECA, the UK's ECGD was established in 1919, most governmental agencies were established after World War II in order to support domestic exports abroad, primarily to developing countries where private sector finance did not want to assume those risks (Stephens 1999). According to Delio Gianturco (2001: 4):

> ECAs have performed the invaluable function of making credit available to many countries where commercial banks and other private lenders are not willing to make transborder loans, and of making credit available to most developing countries at interest rates and repayment periods that are more favorable than alternative private sources of funds.

Developed countries will continue to rely on their ECAs in order to support the export of their domestic goods abroad, especially to the riskier markets of developing countries.

As a case in point, at the time of this writing, US economic sanctions have been partially lifted against two countries: Cuba and Iran. In January 2016, the Obama administration moved to lift restrictions on US financing of exports to Cuba. The shipping of products such as tractors, construction cranes and sanitation equipment can now occur with US banks providing financing for these exports directly, as opposed to routing US goods through a third country (Davis 2016: A6). These changes will result in increased exports of US manufactured goods to Cuba, since now US companies can "sell goods directly to Cuban state-run enterprises and to use credit to do so" (ibid). However, until the US Congress lifts the trade embargo that still restricts most trade and commerce with the country, US companies will still be limited in this area. Ultimately, the US Ex-Im Bank would be providing insurance or guarantees to support trade finance in this area, and this cannot occur until the trade embargo is lifted.

Also in January 2016, US economic sanctions were lifted against Iran as part of the nuclear deal designed to limit Iran's nuclear program. As of February 2016, US firms and Western banks were still not engaging in business transactions with the country since there was some uncertainty about the implications of the US Treasury classification of Iran as a "state sponsor of terrorism." In practice, this means that no money intended for Iran can go through US banks.

However, there were reports that the Iranian government had already begun negotiations with France for orders of Airbus's jets, which were "likely to be partly financed with loans from European export-credit agencies" (Clark and Krauss 2016: A1, B4). This report also noted that a spokesman for Boeing explained that they were "continuing to assess the situation" with regard to Boeing's interest in Iran (ibid). Although, it certainly seems probable that Boeing would be interested in selling its aircraft to Iran if it were permitted under US law. These examples of new, but potentially risky, markets for exports to Cuba and Iran precisely fit the reason why the ECAs were created in the first place. Indeed, comparisons to the situation with the opening of Russia to business and investment in the 1990s after the end of the Soviet Union were cited in this article (Clark and Krauss 2016: A1, B4).

Second, government-supported ECAs will continue to provide finance for manufacturing and large infrastructure projects due to the lack of private sector finance support for these projects. The information provided in Chapter 5 illustrated these trends, especially as they related to problems of the availability of finance surrounding the 2008 financial crisis. Berne Union statistics documented increases in both medium- and longer-term support during the time frame of the crisis. In 2008, medium- and longer-term cover was $154 billion, but by the end of 2009, medium- and longer-term cover had increased to $191 billion, at the time, the highest ever recorded (Morel 2010: 16).

What is surprising, however, was the time it took for perceptions of risk in financing trade to dissipate after the crisis. Berne Union statistics show that medium- and longer-term support had decreased to $173 billion in 2010, but increased sharply again in 2011 to $191 billion. Even by 2012, cover for medium- and longer-term support was $181 billion, much higher than cover support provided in 2008. It was not until 2013 and 2014 that medium- and longer-term cover support declined back to 2008 levels at $161 billion and $167 billion respectively (Berne Union Statistics data). The primary explanation for this trend was attributed to the continued concern about risk in international markets. According to the World Bank's annual Multilateral Investment Guarantee Agency (MIGA) 2013 World Investment and Political Risk report, "[t]he fact that political risk continues to be perceived as an important constraint to investment into developing countries remains a boon for the political risk insurance (PRI) industry" (World Bank 2013: 6). The 2012 ICC Global Survey reported that representatives of 229 banks located in 110 countries identified, "political changes in the Middle East and North Africa, as well as sovereign debt concerns in Europe and the US" as factors that explained why the risk environment remained uncertain

(ICC Global Survey 2012: 9). Therefore, it seems more likely than not to expect medium- and longer-term export credit insurance to remain at relatively high levels in order to lessen the risk by domestic firms of exporting goods to developing countries, and possibly to continue to use this type of insurance for select markets in Europe and the US.

The politics and economics of supporting domestic industry exports

The third explanation as to why the role of government-supported ECAs will increase in the near future is due to their primary objective of increasing domestic industry exports. In fact, while Chapter 5 examined the role of medium- and longer-term financing during the 2008 crisis, short-term financing generally the purview of the private sector, also began to be provided by the ECAs due to liquidity problems during the crisis.

During the 1990s, private insurers had largely taken over the short-term export credit insurance cover from government-supported ECAs for two reasons. First, the short-term market is viewed as less risky than medium- and long-term cover (Kuhn, Horvath and Jarvis 1995: 14). Second, since short-term business is conducted routinely with commercial banks and buyers for consumer goods and raw materials, this business is less complex than medium- or longer-term projects such as capital goods or infrastructure projects. In addition, these decisions also coincided with the belief, by some governments, that if the private sector was covering these risks then there was not a role for government support, at least for short-term cover (Stephens 1999: 32).

Stephens (1999: 33) estimated that by the late 1990s, 85 to 90 percent of short-term export credit insurance business within and beyond the EU were covered by the private sector without governmental involvement. However, as a result of uncertainty during the 2008 crisis, private insurers began to review their risks on insuring export transactions more carefully and reduced credit limits (Morel 2010: 10). In turn, governments believed that the support provided by their ECAs was necessary in order to increase trade. Thus, when private insurers reduced their provision of short-term credit insurance during the 2008 crisis, public ECAs responded by increasing their short-term credit limits (Blackmon 2016).

Finally, the institutional framework of the Paris Club debt rescheduling coupled with the financing arrangements provided by the IMF that allow for accommodations when countries experience problems with repayment will result in increases in the reliance on government-supported ECAs in the future. Indeed, as discussed in Chapter 4, there are discernible benefits for debtor and creditor countries to continue participating in the extension of export credit facilities and rescheduling. Creditor states benefit since ECA financing allows them to support their domestic export industries. Debtor states benefit since rescheduling defers their payments and allows for continued access to trade finance, especially when these countries would not otherwise have access to these sources of finance. To be sure, the repetitive rescheduling process may diminish over time, especially for countries that are able to show progress in managing their debt and are considered to be in a low risk of debt distress.

Broader policy implications of ECA support

Political scientists should be paying more attention to trade finance and the government agencies that support that finance. Two contemporary events illustrate why this is the case. First, the US Ex-Im Bank has once again had problems in securing its reauthorization from Congress, which resulted in its new lending being suspended from July through December 2015. In fact, even though the US Ex-Im Bank was reauthorized for new business in December 2015, as of July 2016, the US Ex-Im Bank can only approve small export deals. This is because the larger export deals, defined as those with a value of over $10 million, require approval by the US Ex-Im Board. Currently, the Board lacks a quorum since there are three empty seats on its five member board; approval of the larger export deals require at least a quorum of three members. The inability to approve the larger transactions has resulted in firms such as Boeing and General Electric deciding to move some of their operations abroad and benefit from the support of other nations' ECAs (Calmes 2016: B1, B2). In addition, these large loans would be needed for export deals of Boeing aircraft to Iran mentioned in the beginning of this chapter. While President Obama has nominated board members, they would need to be confirmed by the Republican Senate, which has been a difficult battle in the current political climate (Calmes 2015: B1, B4; Calmes 2016: B1, B2).

Unfortunately, this situation has been a recurring once since the US Ex-Im Bank first had trouble with reauthorization in 2010. It is important to point out that prior to that, the US Ex-Im Bank had been reauthorized every year since 1935 (it was established in 1934) and largely with bipartisan support. The problems surrounding the US Ex-Im Bank stem from two different viewpoints on the role and importance of the Bank. One perspective espoused by groups critical of government programs more generally, argues that the US Ex-Im Bank interferes with the free market and provides government subsidies to firms (de Rugy and Katz 2015).[1] The alternative perspective, voiced more often from former ECA employees, is that the US Ex-Im Bank provides insurance and guarantees when private sector finance is not available, or is too expensive, thus correcting for a market failure (Gianturco 2001). While the latter is more correct, there is very little being written on the political and economic implications of ECA financing by political scientists.

Indeed, many of the best books on ECAs, and cited in this book, have been written by persons formerly involved with ECAs and are not well known by academics or policy makers. For example, Malcolm Stephens was former Secretary-General of the International Union of Credit and Investment Insurers (the Berne Union) and he was commissioned by the IMF to do some work on ECAs, culminating in *The Changing Role of Export Credit Agencies* (1999). Rita Rodriguez was a former director of the US Ex-Im Bank and she was the editor, with Gary Clyde Hufbauer of *The Ex-Im Bank in the 21st Century: A New Approach?* (2001). Finally, Delio Gianturco served on the board of directors of the US Ex-Im Bank and in his book, *Export Credit Agencies: The Unsung Giants of International Trade and Finance* (2001) he lamented "very few people outside the ECAs knew what an export credit agency was or what it did" (p. vii).

The problems in the US with the US Ex-Im Bank notwithstanding, there are global trends in increasing both the visibility and use of government-supported ECAs. US Ex-Im Bank economists have correctly identified China's growing assertiveness with its ECA, especially in light of the fact that China is not an OECD Participant to the Arrangement (US Export-Import Bank Competitiveness Report 2010: 119–124). Concerns have also been voiced about the high levels of competition from other emerging market ECAs such as those in Brazil and India. Finally, Russia established its own ECA in July 2011.

The second event involves decisions to use the ECAs for officially-backed short-term cover on a selective basis when private insurance cover is not available. For example, from April 2012 to December 31, 2013, the European Commission excluded Greece from the list of marketable risk countries, meaning that European Union ECAs could provide officially-backed short-term cover for exports to Greece due to "the exceptional economic disturbance to the Greek economy and the scarcity of private insurance cover for exports to Greece" (OJC April 21, 2012). The European Commission extended this provision for

Greece until December 31, 2014 due to continuing problems with the Greek economy (Communication from the Commission 2013). Thus, governments may be more likely to rely on the ECAs for officially-backed short-term use again since the connections between short-term export credit insurance and trade will become more important in the future.

Note

1 It should be noted that one of the most prolific writers against US Ex-Im Bank financing, Veronique de Rugy, is a senior research fellow at the Mercatus Center at George Mason University. Diane Katz is a senior research fellow at the Heritage Foundation. The Mercatus Center is listed as a project of the Koch family foundations, of which two of its members, Charles and David Koch, are chief executive and executive vice president of the privately owned Koch Industries, which has "substantial oil and energy interests" (Lohr 2015: A3). Although, Koch Energy Services (a subsidiary of Koch Industries) is unique among other oil and energy firms because they do not have export interests outside of the US for their oil and energy services (they have a presence in Canada and Mexico but not for oil related services) according to their websites (http://kochind.com/kaes/; http://kochind.com/locations/ accessed May 18, 2016). In other words, their firm would not benefit from US Ex-Im Bank financing since they do not engage in international export markets for their products. This is in contrast to other US based oil and energy firms such as Halliburton, Bechtel, Baker-Hughes and Schlumberger who export their products worldwide and would benefit from US Ex-Im Bank financing.

References

Abbott, Kenneth W. and Duncan Snidal. 2010. International Regulation without International Government: Improving IO Performance through Orchestration. *Review of International Organizations* 5: 315–344.

Abel, Gerhard. 1998. The Multilateral Trading System, the Export Credit Arrangement and the WTO. In *The Export Credit Arrangement: Achievements and Challenges 1978–1988, OECD*. Paris: OECD.

Abouharb, M. Rodwan and David Cingranelli. 2006. The Human Rights Effects of World Bank Structural Adjustment Lending, 1981–2000. *International Studies Quarterly* 50(2): 233–262.

Abouharb, M. Rodwan and David Cingranelli. 2007. *Human Rights and Structural Adjustment*. Cambridge: Cambridge University Press.

Altman, Roger. 2009. Globalization in Retreat. *Foreign Affairs* July/August 88(4): 2–7.

Amiti, Mary and David E. Weinstein. 2009. Exports and Financial Shocks. *NBER Working Paper no. 15556*, December 2009.

Andrews, David, Anthony Boote, Syed Rizavi and Sukhwinder Singh. 1999. *Debt Relief for Low-Income Countries: The Enhanced HIPC Initiative*. IMF Pamphlet Series No. 51. Washington, DC: IMF.

Apodaca, Clair and Pamela Blackmon. 2016. Does the Heavily Indebted Poor Countries Initiative (HIPC) Realize its Goal of Poverty Alleviation? *Journal of Poverty Alleviation and International Development* 7(1): 1–38.

Asmundson, Irena, Thomas Dorsey, Armine Khachatryan, Ioana Niculcea and Mika Saito. 2011. *Trade and Trade Finance in the 2008–09 Financial Crisis. IMF Working Paper 11/16*. Washington, DC: International Monetary Fund.

Auboin, Marc. 2009. Restoring Trade Finance During a Period of Financial Crisis: Stock-Taking of Recent Initiatives. *World Trade Organization Staff Working Paper ERSD-2009-16*, December 2009.

Baker, James C. 2003. *Financing International Trade*. Westport, CT: Praeger.

Baldwin, Robert E. and T. Scott Thompson. 1984. The Appropriate Response to Trade Barriers and 'Unfair' Trade Practices in Other Countries. *American Economic Review* 74(2): 271–276.

Beard, Alan J. and Richard M. Thomas. 2006. *Trade Finance Handbook*. Mason, OH: Thompson.
Becker, William H. and William M. McClenahan, Jr. 2003. *The Market, the State, and the Export-Import Bank of the United States, 1934–2000*. Cambridge, UK: Cambridge University Press.
Berne Union. 2009. *Berne Union Yearbook*. London, UK: The Berne Union.
Bhagwati, Jagdish. 2004. *In Defense of Globalization*. Oxford, UK: Oxford University Press.
Bird, Graham and Alistair Milne. 2003. Debt Relief for Low Income Countries: Is it Effective and Efficient? *The World Economy* 26(1): 43–59.
Bird, Graham and Robert Powell. 2009. Debt Relief in Low-Income Countries: Background, Evolution and Effects. In *Finance, Development and the IMF*, edited by James M. Boughton and Domenico Lombardi. Oxford, UK: Oxford University Press.
Birdsall, Nancy, John Williamson and Brian Deese. 2002. *Delivering on Debt Relief: From IMF Gold to a New Aid Architecture*. Washington, DC: Peterson Institute for International Economics.
Birdsall, Nancy, Stijn Claessens and Ishac Diwan. 2003. Policy Selectivity Forgone: Debt and Donor Behavior in Africa. *World Bank Economic Review* 17(3): 409–435.
Blackmon, Pamela. 2007. Divergent Paths, Divergent Outcomes: Linking Differences in Economic Reform to Levels of U.S. Foreign Direct Investment and Business in Kazakhstan and Uzbekistan. *Central Asian Survey* 26(3): 355–372.
Blackmon, Pamela. 2008. Rethinking Poverty Through the Eyes of the International Monetary Fund and the World Bank. *International Studies Review* 10(2): 179–202.
Blackmon, Pamela. 2009. Factoring Gender into Economic Development: Changing the Policies of the IMF and World Bank. *Women's Studies* 38(2): 213–237.
Blackmon, Pamela. 2010. International Economic Institutions and Global Justice. In *The International Studies Encyclopedia*, edited by Robert Denemark, 4021–4034. Chichester, UK: Wiley Blackwell.
Blackmon, Pamela. 2011. *In the Shadow of Russia: Reform in Kazakhstan and Uzbekistan*. East Lansing, MI: Michigan State University Press.
Blackmon, Pamela. 2012. "The Role of Export-Credit Agencies in the 2008 Financial Crisis: Were They Used to Supplement Private Sector Finance and Sustain International Trade?" Paper presented at the Annual Meeting of the International Studies Association, San Francisco, CA, April 1–4, 2012.
Blackmon, Pamela. 2016. OECD Export Credit Agencies: Supplementing Short-term Export Credit Insurance during the 2008 Financial Crisis. *International Trade Journal* 30(4): 295–318.
Bohn, John A. 1985. Governmental Response to Third World Debt: The Role of the Export-Import Bank. *Stanford Journal of International Law* 21: 461–497.

Boorman, Jack. 2006. Dealing Comprehensively, and Justly, with Sovereign Debt. In *Sovereign Debt at the Crossroads*, edited by Chris Jochnick and Fraser A. Preston. Oxford, UK: Oxford University Press.

Booth, David. 2003. Introduction and Overview. *Development Policy Review* 21(2): 131–159.

Borensztein, Eduardo, Eduardo Levy Yeyati and Ugo Panizza. 2006. *Living with Debt: How to Limit the Risks of Sovereign Finance*. Washington, DC: Inter-American Development Bank.

Borscheid, Peter and Niels Viggo Haueter (Eds.) 2012. *World Insurance: The Evolution of a Global Risk Network*. Oxford, UK: Oxford University Press.

Brown, Richard P. C. 1992. The IMF and Paris Club Debt Rescheduling: A Conflicting Role? *Journal of International Development* 4(3): 291–313.

Broz, J. Lawrence and Michael Brewster Hawes. 2006. Congressional Politics of Financing the International Monetary Fund. *International Organization* 60(1): 367–399.

Buckley, Peter J. 1983. Government-Industry Relations in Exporting: Lessons from the United Kingdom. In *Export Promotion: The Public and Private Sector Interaction*, edited by Michael R. Czinkota. New York: Praeger.

Busby, Joshua. 2007. Bono Made Jesse Helms Cry: Jubilee 2000, Debt Relief and Moral Action in International Politics. *International Studies Quarterly* 51(2): 247–275.

Callaghy, Thomas. 2002. *Innovation in the Sovereign Debt Regime: From the Paris Club to Enhanced HIPC and Beyond*. Washington, DC: World Bank Operations Evaluation Department.

Callaghy, Thomas. 2010. The Paris Club, debt and poverty reduction: Evolving patterns of governance. In *Global Governance, Poverty and Inequality*, edited by Jennifer Clapp and Rorden Wilkinson, 162–184. London: Routledge.

Calmes, Jackie. 2015. Ex-Im Bank is Reopened, but Big Loans are Stalled. *The New York Times*, December 8, 2015: B1, B4.

Calmes, Jackie. 2016. Inflexibility of Senator Stymies Ex-Im Bank. *New York Times*, June 28, 2016: B1, B2.

Chauvin, N. and Aart Kraay. 2005. What Has 100 Billion Dollars of Debt Relief Done for Low-Income Countries? Accessed January 12, 2011. http://papers.ssrn.com/sol3/papers.cfm?abstract_id=818504

Cheru, Fantu. 2006. Playing Games with African Lives: The G7 Debt Relief Strategy and the Politics of Indifference. In *Sovereign Debt at the Crossroads*, edited by Chris Jochnick and Fraser A. Preston. Oxford, UK: Oxford University Press.

Chwieroth, Jeffrey. 2008. Normative Change from Within: The International Monetary Fund's Approach to Capital Account Liberalization. *International Studies Quarterly* 52(1): 129–158.

Clark, Ian. 1999. *Globalization and International Relations Theory*. Oxford, UK: Oxford University Press.

Clark, Nicola and Clifford Krauss. 2016. With Sanctions at an End, the West Talks Business and Investment with Iranians. *The New York Times*, January 26, A1, B4.

Cleary, Seamus. 1995. The World Bank and NGOs. In *The Conscious of the World: The Influence of Non-Governmental Organizations in the UN System*, edited by Peter Willetts. Washington, DC: The Brookings Institution.

Cline, William R. 2005. Trade Finance and Financial Crises. In *Access to Trade Finance in Times of Crisis*, edited by Jian-Ye-Wang and Marcio Ronci, 19–23. Washington, DC: IMF.

Cohen, Daniel. 2001. The HIPC Initiative: True and False Promises. *International Finance* 4(3): 363–380.

Copelovitch, Mark. 2010a. Master or Servant? Common Agency and the Political Economy of IMF Lending. *International Studies Quarterly* 54(1): 49–77.

Copelovitch, Mark. 2010b. *The International Monetary Fund in the Global Economy: Banks, Bonds and Bailouts*. Cambridge, UK: Cambridge University Press.

Crockett, A. D. 1992. The International Monetary Fund in the 1990s. *Government and Opposition* 27(3): 267–282.

Czinkota, Michael R. (Ed.) 1983. *Export Promotion: The Public and Private Sector Interaction*. New York: Praeger.

Das, Udaibir, Michael Papaioannou and Magdalena Polan. 2009. Debut Sovereign Bond Issues: Strategic Considerations and Determinants of Characteristics. In *Debt Relief and Beyond*, edited by Carlos A. Primo Braga and Dorte Domeland. Washington, DC: World Bank.

Davis, Julie Hirschfeld. 2016. US Eases Restrictions on Financing Exports and Shipping Goods to Cuba. *The New York Times*, January 27, A6.

de Rugy, Veronique and Diane Katz. 2015. The Export-Import Bank's Top Foreign Buyers. April 15. http://mercatus.org/publication/export-import-bank-s-top-foreign-buyers

de Vries, Jan, van der Woude, Ad. 1997. *The First Modern Economy: Success, Failure, and Perseverance of the Dutch Economy, 1500–1815*. Cambridge, UK: Cambridge University Press.

Dorsey, Thomas. 2009. Trade Finance Stumbles. *Finance & Development*, March 2009: 18–19.

Dreher, Axel and Jan-Egbert Sturm. 2006. Do IMF and World Bank Influence Voting in the UN General Assembly? *CESifo Working Paper Series 1724*, CESifo Group Munich.

Dreher, Axel and Nathan Jensen. 2007. Independent Actor or Agent? An Empirical Analysis of the Impact of US Interests on IMF Conditions. *Journal of Law and Economics* 50(1): 105–124.

Dreher, Axel and Roland Vaubel. 2004. The Causes and Consequences of IMF Conditionality. *Emerging Markets Finance and Trade* 40(3): 26–54.

Dreher, Axel, Jan-Egbert Strum and James Raymond Vreeland. 2013. Politics and IMF Conditionality. *CESifo Working Paper No 4308*.

Dur, Andreas. 2007. Foreign Discrimination, Protection for Exporters, and U.S. Trade Liberalization. *International Studies Quarterly* 51(2): 457–480.

Easterly, William. 2001. Think Again: Debt Relief. *Foreign Policy* 127, 20–26.

Easterly, William. 2002. How Did Heavily Indebted Poor Countries Become Heavily Indebted? Reviewing Two Decades of Debt Relief. *World Development* 30(10): 1677–1696.

Easterly, William. 2005. What did structural adjustment adjust? The Association of policies and growth with repeated IMF and World Bank adjustment loans. *Journal of Development Economics* 76: 1–22.

Easterly, William. 2006. *The White Man's Burden: Why the West's Efforts to Aid the Rest Have Done So Much Ill and So Little Good*. New York: Penguin Publishing.

Eurodad. 2011. *Exporting goods or exporting debts? Export Credit Agencies and the roots of developing country debt*. Brussels: European Commission and EED.

Evans, Peter C. and Kenneth A. Oye. 2001. "International Competition: Conflict and Cooperation in Government Export Financing." In *The Ex-Im Bank in the 21st Century: A New Approach?* edited by Gary Clyde Hufbauer and Rita M. Rodriguez, 113–158. Washington, DC: Institute for International Economics.

Felbermayr, Gabriel, Inga Heiland and Erdal Yalcin. 2012. Mitigating Liquidity Constraints: Public Export Credit Guarantees in Germany. *CESIFO Working Paper no. 3908 Category 8 Trade Policy*, August 2012.

Frieden, Jeffrey. 2006. *Global Capitalism: Its Rise and Fall in the Twentieth Century*. New York: W.W. Norton.

Gamarra, Boris, Malvian Pollock and Carlos A. Primo Braga. 2009. "Debt Relief to Low-Income Countries: A Retrospective." In *Debt Relief and Beyond: Lessons Learned and Challenges Ahead*, edited by Carlos A. Primo Braga and Dorte Domeland, Washington, DC: World Bank. 11–33.

Gianturco, Delio. 2001. *Export Credit Agencies: The Unsung Giants of International Trade and Finance*. Westport, CT: Quorum Books.

Giddens, Anthony. 2000. *Runaway World: How Globalization is Reshaping Our Lives*. New York: Routledge.

Gillespie, A. Ian. 2001. "A Canadian Perspective." In *The Ex-Im Bank in the 21st Century: A New Approach?* edited by Gary Clyde Hufbauer and Rita M. Rodriguez, 227–234. Washington, DC: Institute for International Economics.

Gilman, Martin G. and Jian-Ye Wang. 2003. *Official Financing: Recent Developments and Issues*. Washington, DC: IMF.

Gilpin, Robert. 1994. *Global Political Economy*. Princeton, NJ: Princeton University Press.

Glatzer, Miguel and Dietrich Rueschemeyer. 2005. *Globalization and the Future of the Welfare State*. Pittsburgh, PA: University of Pittsburgh Press.

Grindle, Merilee S. 2004. Good Enough Governance: Poverty Reduction and Reform in Developing Countries. Governance. *An International Journal of Policy, Administration and Institutions* 17(4): 525–548.

Gunter, Bernhard. 2011. Achieving the MDGs and Ensuring Debt Sustainability. *Third World Quarterly* 32(1): 45–63.

Gupta, Sanjeev, Benedict Clements, Maria Teresa Guin-Siu and Luc Leruth. 2004. Debt Relief and Public Health Spending in Heavily Indebted Poor Countries. In *Health and Development: Why Investing in Health is Critical for Achieving Economic Development Goals*. Washington, DC: IMF.

Gupta, In *The Ex-Im Bank in the 21st Century: A New Approach?* edited by Gary Clyde Hufbauer and Rita M. Rodriguez. Washington, DC: Institute for International Economics.

Helleiner, Eric. 2011. Understanding the 2007–2008 Global Financial Crisis: Lessons for Scholars of International Political Economy. *Annual Review of Political Science* 14: 67–87.

Hodgson, Glen. 2005. Trade Credit for Crisis Countries: The Role of Export Credit Agencies. In *Access to Trade Finance in Times of Crisis*, edited by Jian-Ye Wang and Marcio Ronci. Washington, DC: IMF.

Holtom, Duncan. 2007. The Challenge of Consensus Building: Tanzania's PRSP 1998–2001. *The Journal of Modern African Studies* 45(2): 233–251.

Hufbauer, Gary C. and Rita Rodriguez. 2001. Ex-Im Bank: Overview, Challenges, and Policy Options. In *The Ex-Im Bank in the 21st Century A New Approach?* edited by Gary Clyde Hufbauer and Rita Rodriguez. Washington, DC: Institute for International Economics.

Iacovone L. and V. Zavacka. 2009. Banking Crises and Exports. Lessons from the Past. *World Bank Policy Research Working Paper, 5016*. August 2009.

Ilias, Shayerah. 2012. *Reauthorization of the Export-Import Bank: Issues and Policy Options for Congress*. Washington, DC: Congressional Research Service.

Imboela, Bruce L. 2005. Poverty Reduction in Zambia: A Conceptual Analysis of the Zambian Poverty Reduction Strategy Paper. *Bulletin of Science, Technology and Society* 25(5): 435–445.

International Chamber of Commerce (ICC) Global Survey. 2010. *Rethinking Trade and Finance*. Paris, France: International Chamber of Commerce.

International Monetary Fund (IMF). 1998. *Official Financing for Developing Countries*. Washington, DC: IMF.

International Monetary Fund (IMF). 2001. *What is the International Monetary Fund?* Washington, DC: IMF.

International Monetary Fund (IMF). 2009. *Staff Guidance Note on Debt Limits in Fund-Supported Programs*. Washington, DC: IMF.

International Monetary Fund (IMF) and World Bank. 2001. *Debt Relief for Poverty Reduction: The Role of the Enhanced HIPC Initiative*. Washington, DC: IMF and World Bank.

International Monetary Fund (IMF) and World Bank. 2006. *Review of Low-Income Country Debt Sustainability Framework and Implications of the MDRI*. Washington, DC: IMF.

Japanese Bank for International Cooperation (JBIC). Annual Reports 2000–2012.

Kaltenthaler, Karl C., Ronald D. Gelleny and Stephen J. Ceccoli. 2004. Explaining Citizen Support for Trade Liberalization. *International Studies Quarterly* 48(4): 829–852.

Keohane, Robert. 1984. *After Hegemony: Cooperation and Discord in the World Political Economy*. Princeton, NJ: Princeton University Press.

Killick, Tony. 1984. The Impact of Fund Stabilisation Programmes. In *The Quest for Economic Stabilisation: The IMF and the Third World*, edited by Tony Killick. London: Heinemann.

Killick, Tony. 1995. *IMF Programmes in Developing Countries: Design and Impact*. London: Routledge.

Klasen, A. 2011. The Role of Export Credit Agencies in Global Trade. *Global Policy* 2(2): 1–3.

Klein, Thomas. 1987. Debt Relief for African Countries: A New Approach by Official Creditors in the Paris Club. *Finance and Development* 24(4): 10–13.

Krasner, Stephen. 1983. *International Regimes*. Ithaca, NY: Cornell University Press.

Kuhn, Michael. 1994. *Official Financing for Developing Countries*. Washington, DC: International Monetary Fund.

Kuhn, Michael, Balaz Horvath and Christoper J. Jarvis. 1995. *Officially Supported Export Credits: Recent Developments and Prospects*. Washington, DC: IMF.

Lander, Mark and Annie Lowrey. 2012. Obama Bid to Cut the Government Tests Congress. *The New York Times*, January 14, A1.

Letovsky, R. 1990. The Export Finance Wars. *Columbia Journal of World Business* 25, 25–35.

Levit, Janet Koven. 2004. The Dynamics of International Trade Finance Regulation: The Arrangement on Officially Supported Export Credits. *Harvard International Law Journal* 45: 65–182.

Levy, Natan. 2014. "IMF Sidelined in Argentina, Paris Club Accord." Business News Americas May 29, 2014 at http://bnamericas.com/news/banking/imf-sidelined-in-argentina-paris-club-accord

Lohr, Steve. 2015. Dispute over a Bank Threatens a Bank Praised by Obama. *The New York Times*, October 26, A1, A3.

Lora, Eduardo and Mauricio Olivera. 2006. Public Debt and Social Expenditure: Friends or Foes? Washington, DC: *Inter-American Development Bank Working Paper No. 563*.

Mander, Benedict. 2014. Argentina Reaches Landmark Deal with Paris Club Creditors. *Financial Times* May 29, 2014. http://ft.com/cms/s/0/212b0b1e-e722-11e3-aa93-00144feabdc0.html#axzz37SviIfbR

Matthews, Jessica. 1997. Power Shift. *Foreign Affairs* 76(1): 50–66.

McGee, Rosemary, Josh Levene and Alexandra Hughes. 2002. Assessing Participation in Poverty Reduction Strategy Papers: A Desk-Based Synthesis of Experience in Sub-Saharan Africa. *Institute of Development Studies, Research Report 52*.

McGee, Rosemary, Josh Levene and Alexandra Hughes. 2002. Assessing Participation in Poverty Reduction Strategy Papers: A Desk-Based Synthesis of Experience in Sub-Saharan Africa. *Institute of Development Studies, Research Report 52.*

MIGA Staff. 2010. *World Investment and Political Risk 2009*. Washington, DC: World Bank.

Mitrany, David. 1975. *The Functional Theory of Politics*. London: St. Martin's Press for the London School of Economics and Political Science.

Mittelman, James. 2000. *The Globalization Syndrome*. Princeton, NJ: Princeton University Press.

Moran, Theodore. 1999. *Foreign Direct Investment and Development: The New Policy Agenda for Developing Countries and Economies in Transition.* Washington, DC: Institute for International Economics.

Moran, Theodore. 2006. *Harnessing Foreign Direct Investment for Development: Policies for Developed and Developing Countries*. Washington, DC: Center for Global Development.

Moravcsik, Andrew M. 1989. Disciplining Trade Finance: The OECD Export Credit Arrangement. *International Organization* 43(1): 173–205.

Morel, Fabrice. 2010. *Credit Insurance in Support of International Trade: Observations throughout the Crisis*. London: The Berne Union.

Niskanen, William A. (2001) Should Ex-Im Be Retired? In *The Ex-Im Bank in the 21st Century A New Approach?* edited by Gary Clyde Hufbauer and Rita Rodriguez. Washington, DC: Institute for International Economics.

Oatley, Thomas and Jason Yackee. 2004. American Interests and IMF Lending. *International Politics* 41(September): 415–429.

O'Brien, Robert, Anne Marie Goetz, Jan Aart Scholte and Marc Williams. 2000. *Contesting Global Governance: Multilateral Economic Institutions and Global Social Movements*. Cambridge, UK: Cambridge University Press.

Official Journal of the European Union (OJC). 2012. Communication from the Commission amending the Communication of the Commission to the Member States pursuant to Article 93(1) of the EC Treaty applying Articles 92 and 93 of the Treaty to short-term export-credit insurance. April 21.

Organization for Economic Cooperation and Development (OECD). 1998. *The Export Credit Arrangement: Achievements and Challenges 1978–1998*. Paris: OECD.

Organization for Economic Cooperation and Development (OECD). 2003. *Export Credit Financing Systems in OECD Member and Non-Member Countries. 2002 Supplement*. Paris: OECD.

Organization for Economic Cooperation and Development (OECD). 2009. Trade and Agriculture Directorate Participants to the Arrangement on Officially Supported Export Credits. *Officially Supported Export Credits and the Financial Crisis: Measures Taken at the National Level by the Participants to the Arrangement, as at 30 June 2009.*

Organization for Economic Cooperation and Development (OECD). 2010a. Trade and Agriculture Directorate Participants to the Arrangement on Officially Supported Export Credits. *Information Note on the Recently*

Agreed Changes to the Rules on Minimum Premium for Officially Supported Export Credits, June 03.

Organization for Economic Cooperation and Development (OECD). 2010b. OECD Factbook 2010. Accessed April 16, 2015. http://dx.doi.org/10.1787/20743920-2010-table4

Organization for Economic Cooperation and Development (OECD). 2011. Statistics on Resource Flows to Developing Countries, February. OECD.

Organization for Economic Cooperation and Development (OECD) Development Assistance Committee (DAC). 2010. DAC Statistical Reporting Directives. November 12, 2010.

Paris Club. 2001. Press Release. The Paris Club and Ghana Agree to a Debt Restructuring, December 10.

Paris Club. 2002. Press Release. The Paris Club and Ghana Agree to a Debt Restructuring Under the Enhanced Heavily Indebted Poor Countries Initiative, May 16.

Paris Club. 2003. Press Release. The Paris Club Agrees to a Rescheduling of Ecuador's Debt. Accessed May 18, 2012. http://clubdeparis.org/sections/communication/archives-2003/equateur4884/viewLanguage/en

Paris Club. 2004. Press Release. Paris Club Reduces Ghana's Debt under the Enhanced HIPC Initiative, July 22.

Paris Club. 2005. Press Release. The Paris Club Reschedules US$ 137 million of the Dominican Republic's Debt, October 21.

Paris Club. 2006. Press Release. Paris Club Cancel's almost 100% of Cameroon's Debt, June 17.

Paris Club. 2010. "Classification." Accessed July 14, 2011. http://clubdeparis.org/sections/dette-traitee-en-club/categories-de-dette/definition-dettes

Pierson, Warren Lenn. 1940. Export-Import Bank Operations. *Annals of the American Academy of Political and Social Science* 211: 35–40.

Przeworski, Adam and James Raymond Vreeland. 2000. The Effects of IMF Programs on Economic Growth. *Journal of Development Economics* 62: 385–421.

Reich, Robert. 2009. Government in Your Business. *Harvard Business Review*, July 87(7): 94–99.

Reid, Stanley. 1983. Export Research in a Crisis. In *Export Promotion: The Public and Private Sector Interaction*, edited by Michael R. Czinkota. New York: Praeger.

Rieffel, Alexis. 1984. The Paris Club 1978–1983. *Columbia Journal of Transnational Law* 23: 83–110.

Rieffel, Alexis. 1985. *The Role of the Paris Club in Managing Debt Problems*. Princeton, NJ: Princeton University, Essays in International Finance, No. 161.

Rieffel, Lex. 2003. *Restructuring Sovereign Debt: The Case for Ad Hoc Machinery*. Washington, DC: Brookings Institution Press.

Rosenau, James N. 1997. *Along the Domestic-Foreign Frontier: Exploring Governance in a Turbulent World*. Cambridge, UK: Cambridge University Press.

Ruggie, John. 1982. International Regimes, Transactions and Change: Embedded Liberalism in the Postwar Economic Order. *International Organization* 36: 379–415.

Sachs, Jeffrey. 1989. Conditionality, debt relief, and the developing country debt crisis. In Jeffrey Sachs (Ed.) *Developing Country Debt and Economic Performance. Vol. 1: The International Financial System*. Chicago: University of Chicago Press.

Sachs, Jeffrey. 2006. *The End of Poverty: Economic Possibilities for Our Time*. New York: Penguin Press.

Setser, Brad. 2009. The Shape of Things to Come. *Finance and Development* 36–39, March 2009.

Solomon, Deborah, Damian Paletta, Jon Hilsenrath and Aaron Lucchatti. 2008. U.S. to Buy Stakes in Nation's Largest Banks. *The Wall Street Journal*, October 14: A1.

Srinivasan, T.N. 1988. Structural Adjustment, Stabilization and the Poor. Economic Development Institute, World Bank (EDI: Catalogue No. 400/056).

Staff Team from the Japan Bank for International Cooperation. 2005. The JBIC Financing Facility for Indonesia, in *Access to Trade Finance in Times of Crisis*, edited by Jian-Ye Wang and Marcio Ronci. Washington, DC: IMF.

Starr, Piper. 2005. The U.S. Export-Import Bank and the Asian Crisis. In *Access to Trade Finance in Times of Crisis*, edited by Jian-Ye Wang and Marcio Ronci. Washington, DC: IMF.

Stephens, Malcolm. 1999. *The Changing Role of Export Credit Agencies*. Washington, DC: International Monetary Fund.

Stewart, Frances. 1995. *Adjustment and Poverty: Options and Choices*. London: Routledge.

Stewart, Frances and Michael Wang. 2006. Do PRSPs Empower Poor Countries and Disempower the World Bank or is it the Other Way Round? In *Globalization and the Nation State: The Impact of the IMF and World Bank* (pp. 111–142), edited by Gustav Ranis, James Raymond Vreeland and Stephen Kosack. London: Routledge.

Stiglitz, Joseph. 2002. *Globalization and Its Discontents*. New York: W. W. Norton.

Stiglitz, Joseph. 2007. *Making Globalization Work*. New York: W.W. Norton.

Stone, Randall. 2004. The Political Economy of IMF Lending in Africa. *American Political Science Review* 98(4): 577–591.

Stone, Randall. 2008. The Scope of IMF Conditionality. *International Organization* 62(4): 589–620.

Stone, Randall. 2011. *Controlling Institutions: International Organizations and the Global Economy*. Cambridge, UK: Cambridge University Press.

Stolper, Wolfgang and Paul Samuelson. 1941. Protection and Real Wages. *Review of Economic Studies* 9: 58–73.

Summers, Lawrence. 2001. Continuing the Fight against International Trade Finance Subsidies. In *The Ex-Im Bank in the 21st Century. A New Approach?* edited by Gary Hufbauer and Rita Rodriguez. Washington, DC: Institute for International Economics.

Thacker, Strom. 1999. The High Politics of IMF Lending. *World Politics* 52(October): 38–75.

United Kingdom Export Credit and Guarantees Department (ECGD). Annual Report 2000–2001–2011–2012.

United Kingdom Export Credit and Guarantees Department (ECGD). Annual Report 2004–2005; 2005–2006; 2008–2009.

United Kingdom Export Credit and Guarantees Department (ECGD). Annual Review and Resource Accounts 2004–2005; 2005–2006; 2008–2009. Great Britain: ECGD.

United Nations Development Program (UNDP). Annual Report 2004. New York: UNDP.

United States Export-Import Bank Annual Reports. 2002; 2004; 2005–2007; 2010. Washington, DC: U.S. Export-Import Bank.

United States Export-Import Bank Annual Reports. 2000–2012. Washington, DC: U.S. Ex-Im Bank.

United States Export-Import Bank Annual Reports. *Competitiveness Reports 2003, 2007–2010*. Washington, DC: U.S. Export-Import Bank.

United States Export-Import Bank Annual Reports. 2004; 2005. Washington, DC: U.S. Ex-Im Bank.

Van der Veer, K.J.M. 2011. Private Trade Credit Insurers during the Crisis: The Invisible Bankers. In *Trade Finance During the Great Trade Collapse* (pp. 199–212), edited by J.P. Chauffour and M. Malouche. Washington, DC: World Bank.

Vauble, Roland. 1986. A Public Choice Approach to International Organization. *Public Choice* 51: 39–57.

Vaubel, Roland. 1991. Problems at the IMF. *Swiss Review of World Affairs* 40: 20–22.

Vaubel, Roland. 1996. Bureaucracy at the IMF and the World Bank: A Comparison of the Evidence. *The World Economy* 19: 195–210.

Vreeland, James Raymond. 2003. Why Do Governments and the IMF Enter Into Agreements? Statistically Selected Cases. *International Political Science Review* 24(3): 321–343.

Vreeland, James Raymond. 2007. *The International Monetary Fund: Politics of Conditional Lending*. London: Routledge.

Wang, Jian-Ye and Marcio Ronci. 2005. *Access to Trade Finance in Times of Crisis*. Washington, DC: IMF.

Wang, Jian-Ye and Helaway Tadesse. 2005. Overview. In *Access to Trade Finance in Times of Crisis*, edited by Jian-Ye Wang and Marcio. Ronci. Washington, DC: International Monetary Fund.

Weaver, Catherine and Ralf J. Leiteritz. 2005. Our Poverty is a World Full of Dreams: Reforming the World Bank. *Global Governance* 11: 369–388.

Weber, Heloise. 2004. Reconstituting the "Third World"? Poverty Reduction and Territorality in the Global Politics of Development. *Third World Quarterly* 25(1): 187–206.

Weisman, Steven. 2006. IMF Votes to Enhance Power of China and Others. *The New York Times*, September 19, C4.

Weiss, John. 2008. The Aid Paradigm for Poverty Reduction: Does it Make Sense? *Development Policy Review* 26(4): 407–426.
Willett, Thomas. 2006. The IMF and Capital Account Crises: The Case for a Lender of Last Resort and Conditionality Functions. In *Globalization and the Nation State: The Impact of the IMF and the World Bank*, edited by Gustav Ranis, James Raymond Vreeland and Stephen Kosack. New York: Routledge.
Williams, Lydia. 1999. Women's Eyes on the World Bank: Integrating Gender Equity into Advocacy Work. In *Gender Works: Oxfam Experience in Policy and Practice*, edited by Fenella Porter, Ines Smyth and Caroline Sweetman. United Kingdom: Oxfam.
Woods, Ngaire. 2003. The United States and the International Financial Institutions: Power and Influence within the World Bank and the IMF. In *US Hegemony and International Organizations*, edited by Rosemarie Foot, S. MacFarlane and M. Mastanduno. Oxford, UK: Oxford University Press.
Woods, Ngaire. 2006. *The Globalizers: The IMF, the World Bank, and Their Borrowers*. New York: Cornell University Press.
World Bank. 2012. *Global Development Finance: External Debt of Developing Countries*. Washington, DC: World Bank.
World Bank, MIGA. 2013. *World Investment and Political Risk*. Washington, DC: World Bank.
World Trade Organization. 2008. *Experts Discuss Problems of Trade Finance*. WTO News Item 12 November 2008.
World Trade Organization. 2009; 2010. *International Trade Statistics*.
World Trade Organization. 2013. *World Trade Report*.
Wright, Christopher. 2011. Export Credit Agencies and Global Energy: Promoting National Exports in a Changing World. *Global Policy* 2(SI): 133–143.

Index

For Product Safety Concerns and Information please contact our EU representative GPSR@taylorandfrancis.com Taylor & Francis Verlag GmbH, Kaufingerstraße 24, 80331 München, Germany